Look Who's Talking!

Strategies for Developing Group Interaction

ORAL FLUENCY PRACTICE
FOR GRADES FIVE THROUGH ADULT

Mary Ann Christison
Snow College
Ephraim, Utah USA

Sharron Bassano
University of California Extension
Santa Cruz, California USA

Alta Book Center Publishers
San Francisco, California 94010 USA

Project Editor: Helen Munch
Production/Design: E. Carol Gee
Cover Art: Helen Daniels

The illustration on pages 102 and 103 is by
Kathleen B. Peterson and is from *PURPLE COWS & POTATO CHIPS*
by Mary Ann Christison and Sharron Bassano.
Copyright 1995 by Alta Book Center Publishers.

Alta Book Center Publishers—San Francisco
14 Adrian Court
Burlingame, California 94010 USA
Phone: 800 ALTA/ESL • 650.692.1285
Fax: 800 ALTA/FAX • 650.692.4654
Email: info@altaesl.com • WWW.ALTAESL.COM

ISBN 1-882483-33-2

Printed in the United States of America

Contents

* These activities have corresponding duplicatable student exercise sheets.
  Consult the appropriate Notes to the Teacher for the correct page references.

Contents Continued

* These activities have corresponding duplicatable student exercise sheets.
  Consult the appropriate Notes to the Teacher for the correct page references.

Traditional approaches to language teaching have usually involved students in activities that are only indirectly related to actual language use. Activities such as drills, memorization, producing short answers, or answering questions about stories generally require students to adopt someone else's meaning, either the teacher's or an author's. Many hours have been spent on rote or non-meaningful activities partly because of custom and partly because of a lack of suitable materials or alternatives.

Look Who's Talking! Second Edition recognizes that teachers need direct, meaningful classroom activities and that students need active, structured experience in their new language. In the five years since the first edition was published, both research and practice in language teaching have provided teachers with increasing evidence of the central role that meaning-based activities play in language learning. In this new edition, the numerous controlled activities and the strategies for implementing them expand on what has been proven right in the first edition.

The authors of this very successful teacher resource would be the first to agree that a book is only one of the many resources a good teacher can use to give students what they need. But as a teacher resource, *Look Who's Talking!* is one of the best books available.

Karl J. Krahnke
Colorado State University

Why We Wrote This Book

Ask any student of English as a second language what he or she wants most from the classroom experience, and nine times out of ten the answer will be, "More conversation practice!"

As teachers aware of the input that students receive both in and out of class, we have often experimented with group interaction activities in the classroom. Sometimes our experiments have succeeded and sometimes they have not. We believe that when group work fails, it is neither because of the activity itself nor because the teacher is ill-prepared. Rather, the problem lies with unrealistic performance expectations. We expect our students to be well versed in the fundamentals of group dynamics and to know how to handle the more vocal or shy members in a group.

What we propose as a solution are (1) specific strategies to prepare students to interact democratically and independently in different situations and (2) progressive sequencing of activities. Specific strategies enable students to learn functional interaction techniques while simultaneously building group spirit and trust. Careful sequencing involves movement from low-risk, non-personal topics to higher-risk, personal topics.

About This Book

The 78 group interaction activities in *Look Who's Talking! Second Edition* are organized around the six different strategies described on pp. viii & ix. The activities are designed for secondary and adult school students of English at the intermediate to advanced levels.

Each of the six strategies and its corresponding activities are presented as a unit. All units begin with Notes to the Teacher describing each activity, its focus (non-personal or personal), the time needed to complete the activity, and any necessary materials. Following the notes are duplicatable student exercise sheets for use with specific activities in that unit. The exercise sheets may be copied repeatedly for classroom use. In many cases, the exercise sheets serve as *models* only. We encourage you to adapt activities or exercise sheets to the specific content of your class or course and to the interests, concerns, and abilities of your students.

The six strategies we have identified and worked with in developing our group interaction activities are restructuring, one-centered, unified group, dyad, small group, and large group. A complete description of each strategy and its objectives follows.

Strategy Descriptions

**Strategy 1
Restructuring**

Objectives
- To break down the traditional teacher-controlled classroom
- To create opportunities for supportive behavior
- To dispel fears and anxieties
- To relax both the students and the teacher

Restructuring activities usually require students to get up from their chairs and to interact physically as a group. There is minimal direction by the teacher. In fact, in most activities the teacher is a full participant, the same as any student. Often the communication is through actions, drawings, or quickly written statements. Content may be either personal or non-personal.

**Strategy 2
One-Centered**

Objectives
- To provide each student with individual attention and acceptance from the entire group
- To increase the likelihood of contributions from each student in follow-up discussions

One-centered activities always put one student in the spotlight for a short time on a voluntary basis. Depending on the student's self-confidence, he or she may participate in front of the class or from his or her seat. There is minimal teacher direction. Content may be either personal or non-personal.

**Strategy 3
Unified Group**

Objectives
- To develop cooperation among group members
- To emphasize each student's value to the group
- To provide opportunities for group success

Unified group activities require the participation of each group member. No one may bow out since each student's contribution is essential for completion of the activity. The teacher is only minimally engaged. Content may be either personal or non-personal.

Strategy 4
Dyad

Objectives

- To provide each student with opportunities for simple interaction with one other class member at a time
- To develop sincere interpersonal communication in the second language

Dyad activities allow students to work one-on-one with others in the class. The teacher acts as an observer, assisting as needed. Through dyad activities, students become better acquainted, learn to relax, and develop important personal relationships that will facilitate later group work. Content may be either personal or non-personal.

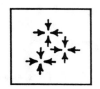 **Strategy 5**
Small Group

Objectives

- To develop in each student a growing sense of commitment to the group
- To develop trust and cooperation among group members
- To develop techniques that facilitate fair group interaction

Small group activities are loosely structured and require patience and good listening habits. They demand attention-sharing, turn-taking, and fair interruptions. The teacher is sometimes a facilitator as well as a participator. Content may be either personal or non-personal.

 Strategy 6
Large Group

Objectives

- The objectives for large groups are the same as those for small groups. The only difference is the inclusion of a larger number and a broader range of students whom the individual group member has learned to trust.

Large group activities are also loosely structured and demand fair group interaction even more strongly than do small group activities because of the larger number of students interacting. The teacher can be a facilitator as well as a participator. Content may be either personal or non-personal.

Introduction

How to Use This Book

There are no hard and fast rules to follow for introducing your students to the strategies. However, we recommend that you begin with the restructuring, one-centered, and unified group strategies as they focus on the students' individual self-images, their attitudes toward learning, and the importance of group cooperation in creating a positive outcome. Once your students appear ready to function in dyads and small groups, you may still want to return occasionally to the earlier strategies to remind students of the advantages of establishing group cooperation and/or of focusing attention on a particular student.

While the activities that demonstrate a specific strategy can be presented in any order, we remind you that the focus of an activity may be either non-personal or personal in terms of its content. In selecting an appropriate activity for your class, try to be sensitive to cultural backgrounds, personalities and class rapport so that maximum student performance and interaction will result. Once you have selected an activity, follow this general procedure:

1. Read the Strategy Descriptions (see pp. viii & ix) and the Notes to the Teacher for the activity you have chosen.
2. Assemble any necessary materials and duplicate student copies of the appropriate exercise sheet(s), as needed.
3. Set up the classroom and have students form dyads or groups according to the strategy you are using.
4. Explain the activity using your teacher notes or distribute copies of the exercise sheet(s). Read the directions aloud or have students read them silently. Answer any questions.
5. Tell students how much time they will have to complete an activity and/or its exercise sheet(s).
6. Leave enough time at the end of class for clean up and any concluding remarks about the activity.

A Final Word

Look Who's Talking! Second Edition offers a wide variety of stimulating, relevant, and fun activities for successful classroom conversation and group interaction. Many of these activities are our own creations; others have been adapted especially to fit the language acquisition focus of this book.

It is not our intention to claim as our own all the ideas in this book. Rather, we hope that in compiling and presenting these activities in a particular framework—through six interaction strategies—we are providing you with the key to fail-proof group interaction and conversation classes.

We wish you success and satisfaction!

> Mary Ann Christison
> Sharron Bassano

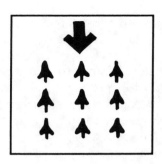

Strategy 1
Restructuring

Strategy 1
Restructuring Activities

Everybody Votes
    Focus: personal
    Time: 20 minutes
    Materials: sheets of newsprint (23" x 27");
        tape;
        colored pens

Hang several sheets of newsprint around the room, each sheet headed with a general conversation topic, such as Politics, Religion, Family, Fun and Recreation, Love and Romance, Work, Friendship. Ask students to consider their most favorite conversation topic and to go stand by the sheet that best represents their choice. After noting the balance of interests, ask students to go stand by the sheet that best represents their least favorite conversation topic.

Once students are aware of one anothers' interests, distribute the colored pens. Ask students to write a personal comment on each of the newsprint sheets about the indicated conversation topic. Continue the activity until everyone has had a chance to write something on every sheet and to read the other comments.

As a wrap-up, reconvene the class and ask students how they felt doing the activity, what things they noticed, what comments they heard. Or have students work in small groups to comment on what they didn't agree with, what they felt compelled to write, and so on.

This activity may be organized around any number of topics, such as Plans for a Saturday Night, Vacation Spots, Things We Can't Live Without, Household Chores, Classroom Activities, and so on.

Introductions
    Focus: personal
    Time: 20 minutes
    Materials: light-colored or white paper (12" x 18");
        colored pens or pencils;
        tape or straight pins

Distribute the paper, one sheet per student, and the colored pens or pencils. Then read the following directions:

Draw a picture of yourself that shows how you feel today, or draw a picture of yourself that shows where you'd rather be, with whom, and what you'd rather be doing. Under the picture write three words ending with -*ing* that tell what you do very well. Above the picture write your name.

Allow five or six minutes for completion of the drawings. Then ask students to tape or pin their drawings to the front of their clothing and to move about the classroom silently, getting acquainted with one another by using only their eyes. After a few minutes, direct students to stop in place and to think about answers to these questions:

Did you see anything similar to your drawing?
Did you see something very different from your drawing?
What did you see that interested you?
With whom would you like to talk?
Was there anything you didn't understand?

Direct the students to move about the room again, asking questions of one another or making comments about the drawings, pointing out similarities or differences. At the end of the activity, have each student choose a partner to interview.

Question Mill
    Focus: non-personal
    Time: 15 minutes
    Materials: magazine pictures;
        tape or straight pins

Tape or pin a magazine picture to each student's back without letting him or her see the picture. Have students move about the classroom asking each other Yes/No questions about their pictures (for example, "Am I a machine?" "Am I an animal?" "Am I something to eat?"). Make sure students ask only Yes/No questions and that they answer only "Yes" or "No" to those questions. After 10 minutes of questions and answers, find out which students know who or what they are.

Line Ups

Focus: personal
Time: 15 minutes
Materials: pictures, word or name cards
for the asterisked (*) items below

Have students line up across the room according to one of the arrangements below. Tell students that they will need to ask one another questions in order to determine their respective positions in line. Present the following two examples:

- last name (or first) in alphabetical order
(*Example:* What is your last/first name?)
- time in the United States
(*Example:* How long have you been in the United States?)
- number of brothers and sisters
- time students got up that morning
- time students went to bed the night before
- birth date (month and day only)
- amount of pocket change each student has
- distance from school to present home
- number of hours from student's country to the students' adopted city
- names of the 50 states in alphabetical order*
- names of the slowest to fastest animals (or forms of transportation)*
- names of the smallest and largest animals
- costs of different items*
- months of the year (or days of the week)

Circle Topics

Focus: non-personal to personal
Time: 20-30 minutes
Materials: a list of conversation topics

Before beginning this activity, you and/or your students will need to create a list of suitable conversation topics. Be sure to include a variety of issues from safe (low-threat) to more volatile (risky). Here are some topics that we've used with different age groups:

Adults	Young Adults
dogs	parents
shoes	allowance
x-rated movies	Saturday
oceans	cars
diet	drugs
the government	pets
vacations	the future
religion	school
family	snacks
garage sales	TV
feminism	sports
nuclear weapons	girlfriends/boyfriends
unions	brothers and sisters
clothing	rock 'n' roll
immigration	clothes
marriage	movies

Have students form two concentric circles so that each student faces a partner. Explain that you will announce a conversation topic and that students in the outer circle will have 30 seconds to state their opinions, ideas, or experiences with that topic to their partner in the inner circle. When the time is up, allow the inner circle students 30 seconds to do the same thing.

At an agreed-upon signal, have the outer circle students move clockwise to a new partner. Then announce a new topic and repeat the activity. Continue until all students are once again facing their original partners.

At this point, ask students to make one more complete rotation of the circle, this time repeating to each partner what they remember being told the first time around by that person. (If students can't remember, their partner should be able to remind them.)

How Well Do You Know Me?
Focus: personal
Time: 20 minutes
Materials: pens or pencils;
exercise sheet, p. 7

Use the exercise sheet provided or make one of your own, listing things that may be true about any given student in the class (for example, *has brown hair; likes chocolate ice cream*). Make certain to include things that students can observe about each other (*has brown hair*) as well as things that they cannot observe and will need to ask about (*likes chocolate ice cream*). Let the composition and interests of your class guide you in creating the descriptions.

Move all furniture from the center of the room so that students can walk about freely. Then distribute copies of the exercise sheet and the pens or pencils and explain the directions. Allow 10 minutes for the activity itself and extra time to check signatures. A prize for the winner adds a nice touch.

What Are You Wearing?
Focus: personal
Time: 10 minutes
Materials: small slips of paper;
a paper bag;
pens or pencils;
exercise sheet, p.8

Distribute two slips of paper to each student and the pens or pencils. Ask students to write on one of the slips a brief description of one item they are wearing that others in the class can see. Tell students to describe the item carefully and clearly (for example, *"I am wearing a gold ring on the small finger of my left hand."*).

Mix all the slips together in a paper bag and have each student draw out a slip. (Be sure that students don't draw their own description!) When everyone has a slip, distribute copies of the exercise sheet. Ask students to find the person wearing the item described on their slip of paper and to get answers to the questions on the exercise sheet.

Repeat the activity asking students to write a description of what *another* student is wearing. Then assemble all the students in a large group or circle. Go stand by one student and ask the first question on the exercise sheet. One of the students who has interviewed that student should be able to provide the correct information. Continue around the room until everyone has had a chance to answer a question.

Where's My Answer?
Focus: non-personal
Time: 10 minutes
Materials: a paper bag;
exercise sheets, pp. 9–11

Use the exercise sheets provided, or prepare a list of similar questions that can be answered easily by your students and write the answers on a separate sheet of paper. (There should be enough questions for everyone in the class.) Cut the sheets so that each question and its answer appear on separate slips of paper. Mix all the questions and answers together thoroughly in a paper bag. Then read the following directions to your students:

I am going to pass around a paper bag. Take a slip of paper from the bag and don't look at it until I tell you to. On the slip of paper is a question or an answer. If you have a question, try to find the person in the class who has the matching answer. If you have an answer, try to find the person who has the matching question. As soon as you have found your question or answer, stand by the person who gave it to you. You will have three minutes to find your match.

Repeat the activity using different questions and answers and/or have students repeat the questions and answers out loud to see if everyone agrees on the responses.

This activity may also be done using matching cards. Here are some suggestions for matches for students of different proficiency levels:

words and pictures
sentences and pictures
paragraphs and pictures
synonyms—words or pictures
antonyms—words or pictures
pictures cut in half (student with top half of picture looks for student with bottom half)
content questions about geography, history, health, science, and so on.
vocabulary—words and their definitions
idiomatic expressions and their definitions
math word problems and their answers
signs/symbols and their meanings
present-and-past tense verbs

Writing Back

Focus: personal
Time: 15 minutes
Materials: paper;
tape or straight pins;
pens or pencils

Have students initially work in pairs. Distribute the pens or pencils and tape or pin a blank sheet of paper to each student's back. Explain that students will have one minute to ask each other questions. At the end of that time, at a given signal from you, each student should write on his or her partner's sheet a one- or two-word response to something learned during the conversation. Then repeat the activity until students have exchanged information and written comments with 6 to 10 other students in the class. Be sure to limit the question/conversation sessions to one minute and to repeat the established signal so that students know when to stop writing and move on.

When the activity has been completed, have students remove the comment sheets from each other's backs. Allow time for students to read the sheets, ask questions, and discuss the comments in a large group sharing.

Riddle Match

Focus: non-personal
Time: 15 minutes
Materials: a paper bag;
exercise sheet, p. 12

This activity is the same as *Where's My Answer?* (p. 5) only the content here, as the title suggests, is riddles instead of questions.

Use the exercise sheet provided or make up your own sheets of riddles and answers (enough for everyone in the class). Cut the sheets so that each riddle and its answer appear on separate slips of paper. Mix the riddles and answers together in a paper bag and have each student draw a slip of paper from the bag. Students with riddles seek out students with answers and vice versa. Be sure that everyone understands that the objective is to talk about the content, not to read it!

At the end of the activity, reconvene the class for a large group sharing of riddles and answers. Clarify any misunderstandings about the humor of the riddles and ask students to share riddles from their native languages or cultures.

How Well Do You Know Me?

Directions: Read the descriptions below. Look around you to see which students in your class match the descriptions. Ask those students to sign their names next to the descriptions. If you can't *see* a match, *ask* several students for information until you find one who can sign his or her name next to the description. The person with the most signatures is the winner.

1. has brown eyes _____

2. likes chocolate ice cream _____

3. is married _____

4. wears glasses _____

5. has dimples _____

6. has a birthday in the same month as yours _____

7. is wearing a watch _____

8. is wearing white socks _____

9. has more than four brothers and sisters _____

10. has been in the United States less time than you have _____

11. has the same first initial as yours _____

12. has a moustache _____

13. drinks apple juice _____

14. does *not* like hamburgers _____

15. is wearing stripes _____

What Are You Wearing?

Directions: Find the person described on your strip of paper. Ask him or her the following questions. Listen carefully. You need to remember the answers! No writing, please.

1. What is your name?

2. Where are you from?

3. How long have you been in the United States?

4. How did you get here? How long was your trip?

5. How old are you?

6. Do you have any family in the United States?

7. What do you miss most?

8. What did you bring in your suitcase that is very important to you?

9. What do you like to do when you are not working or studying?

10. Have you been to any other countries or to any other states in the United States?

Look Who's Talking! ©1995 by Alta Book Center Publishers
Permission is granted to reproduce this page for classroom use.

Where's My Answer?

Directions to the teacher: Duplicate this exercise sheet
and pp. 10-11. Then follow the activity directions in the
Notes to the Teacher, p. 5.

What country is north of the United States?	Canada
Who is the President of the United States?	Bill Clinton
How many states are in the United States?	50
What country is south of the United States?	Mexico
In what month is Christmas celebrated?	December
In what state is Los Angeles?	California
In what state is New York City?	New York
In what state is Chicago?	Illinois
What is the capital of the United States?	Washington, D.C.

Continued

Where's My Answer? Continued

What is the longest river in the United States?	the Mississippi
In what month is Thanksgiving celebrated?	November
In what month is Valentine's Day?	February
In what state are Reno and Las Vegas?	Nevada
Is Florida in the South or North?	South
What is the largest state in the United States?	Alaska
What state is made up of several islands?	Hawaii
Which city is farther west – Reno or Los Angeles?	Reno
In what month is Independence Day celebrated in the United States?	July
How many days are there in May?	31
How many pounds are in one kilogram?	2.2
How many cups of flour do you need to make an average cake?	about 2
How many miles are there in a marathon race?	about 26

Continued

How many inches make one meter?	39
How many minutes are there in one day?	1,440
How many hours are there in one week?	168
How many stars are there in the sky?	Nobody knows!
How many players are there on a football team?	11
How much is 136 and 163?	299
How many days are there in a leap year?	366
How many weeks are there in one year?	52
How many kilometers equal 1 mile?	1.61
How many hours does it take to fly from San Francisco to New York?	about six
How many quarts are there in 4 gallons?	16
How many rows of whiskers does a cat have?	4
How many innings are there in a baseball game?	nine

Riddle Match

Directions to the teacher: Duplicate this exercise sheet .
Then follow the directions in the Notes to the Teacher, p. 6.

- -

Why was the box of writing paper on the desk not moving?

- -

Because it was stationery.

- -

Why do radio announcers have small hands?

- -

Wee paws for station identification.

- -

What has four wheels and flies?

- -

a garbage truck

- -

What is the difference between a radio and a clothesline?

- -

A radio draws the waves and a clothesline waves the drawers.

- -

What has four eyes but cannot see?

- -

Mississippi

- -

What is round on the ends and high in the middle?

- -

Ohio

- -

What runs but has no legs or feet?

- -

a clock or a river

- -

How far can you walk into a forest?

- -

Halfway; in the other half, you're on your way out.

- -

What is black and white and read all over?

- -

a newspaper

- -

What is a definition of "illegal"?

- -

a sick bird

- -

Strategy 2
One-Centered

What Am I?
> Focus: non-personal
> Time: 10-20 minutes
> Materials: 3" x 5" index cards;
> a pen; tape or straight pins

On 20 (or more) index cards, write the names of animals or objects. The names can range from easy or common—*tree, grass, cat, dog*—to more difficult and uncommon—*juicer, backrest, penguin, cockatoo.*

Ask a student to come to the front of the class and stand with his or her back to the other students. Select a card, show it to the rest of the class, and tape or pin it to the student's back. The student then becomes that animal or object and must ask the rest of the class no more than 10 questions about his or her identity. Each question should be asked of a different student who may give only the information requested. If the student does not guess who he or she is after 10 questions, the other students may offer hints. Introduce two or three cards per class session and make certain everyone understands the rules.

A variation of this activity is to show only the selected student the name on the card and make the rest of the class guess what the animal or object is, using Yes/No questions only. This is a very painless, low-risk way to allow shyer, less verbal students to "shine" in class.

Teachers
> Focus: personal
> Time: 30 minutes
> Materials: chalkboard and chalk

Ask students to think about teachers they have had during their lives, including some from outside school (friends or relatives, for example, who have "taught" the students something). Give the class a few minutes to think about the skills their teachers had and what those teachers taught them. Have students share their ideas and examples.

Then ask students to think about their own personal skills and what they themselves could teach someone else. Offer a few examples: one's native language or cuisine, a sport like soccer, or an art form like origami. After a few minutes, go around the class asking each student what he or she could teach someone else and who taught them the skill. List all the students' skills on the board and propose a students' skills-sharing day in the future.

If time permits, wrap up the activity with a short composition on the topic My Best Teacher, or assign the topic for homework. Emphasize again that a teacher may be someone other than a classroom instructor.

Experiences
> Focus: personal
> Time: 15 minutes
> Materials: chalkboard and chalk;
> paper;
> pens or pencils

This activity can be done in one of several ways using the following incomplete sentences written on the board:

A good thing that happened to me today was . . .

A bad thing that happened to me today was . . .

Allow students three minutes to think about the sentences. Then ask students to complete the sentences in writing, either as statements alone or in the form of a letter to you.

Another way to do the activity is to divide students into small groups. Each student has two minutes to share his or her good and bad experiences with the others in the group. Let students know when their time is up.

A third way to do the activity is to have individual students volunteer to share their good and bad experiences with the rest of the class. Encourage students to talk about the feelings they had during their experiences and allow plenty of time for comments, questions, and individual self-expression.

I Am

Focus: personal
Time: 10-20 minutes
Materials: chalkboard and chalk;
paper; pens or pencils

Distribute the paper, pens or pencils and ask students to number on their papers from 1 to 10. Next, write the following two words on the board and ask each student to complete the sentence 10 times:

I am . . .

Do not give any models or sample sentences. Just see what answers students produce.

Invite one or more student volunteers to come to the front of the class, leaving their papers behind. Allow the other students to question the volunteers about their identities (for example, "Who are you?" "Who else are you?" "Are you anyone else?"). Ask the student volunteers to tell the class which role they each liked best, which they felt was most important at that moment, which role they wished they didn't have.

Expand the activity into a writing or small group exercise in which students share their feelings about their different roles and when and with whom they perform them. Point out the difference between students' outer-directed identities (those involving other people) and inner-directed ones (those kept hidden from others). Use the distinction as the basis for an in-class or at-home writing exercise.

True or False

Focus: personal
Time: 10-20 minutes
Materials: chalkboard and chalk;
paper; pens or pencils

Make a list of six statements about yourself, at least two of which are true. Read the statements aloud one at a time to the class and have students guess whether they are true or false. (If you don't want to embarrass yourself, keep the statements innocuous, and share the correct answers before continuing the activity.)

Distribute the paper and the pens or pencils and have students, working in groups of three to five, write down six things about themselves, two of which are true. Following your example, students should read their statements to each other and guess which ones are true and which ones false. Allow students about two minutes each to read. Once the small group sharing is over, reconvene the class and have students share some interesting facts about one another. Make sure students know ahead of time that the information they reveal in their small groups will be shared later on with the rest of the class.

On Focus

Focus: personal
Time: 15 minutes
Materials: exercise sheets, pp. 19–20

This activity can be performed by students working either as a class or in groups of four students each. The basic procedure remains the same for both. Use the exercise sheets provided or prepare similar question handouts. Distribute copies of both pages and review the activity directions.

Invite a student to be the focus person and to sit in a chair in front of the class (or have students select a focus person in their groups). Allow the other students to question the focus person for eight minutes. Students may ask questions from their exercise sheets or pose their own questions. The focus person may refuse to answer a question by stating "I pass" if he or she doesn't know the answer or doesn't want to respond. At the end of the time limit, the focus person may ask any three students any three questions that he or she was asked to answer. Be sure that students understand that there is a time limit, that the focus person has the right to say "I pass," and that the focus person will be allowed to switch the focus back to other students by asking them three of their own questions.

With small groups, limit the questioning time to two minutes and the switch of focus to one question and one student. Allow enough time for each student to be the focus person. Ask students to concentrate on their listening habits—to notice when they want to interrupt, when they want to suggest answers to their own questions, or when they want to take the focus away from someone else. To facilitate the focus switching, use a little bell or some other signal so that all groups finish at approximately the same time.

The Catch-All Bag
Focus: non-personal
Time: 25 minutes
Materials: 16–20 numbered household items in a shopping bag; pens or pencils; a large table; exercise sheet, p. 21

For this activity you will need to fill a "catch-all bag" with 16 to 20 numbered household items. Using the exercise sheet provided, prepare an unnumbered list of all the items. (Be sure the items are listed out of numerical order.)

Display all the items on a large table and distribute copies of the exercise sheet. Review the activity directions and allow students 10 minutes to match the numbered items to the names on the list. Encourage comments and discussion. After 10 minutes, have students identify each of the numbered objects by name and check their answers.

If this activity is done in small groups, give each group an exercise sheet and a separate bag with an equal number of items. Have students take turns identifying the items by number until everyone has had a turn. Then have the groups switch bags so that they have a chance to work with other items on the list. If a student in a group incorrectly identifies an item, the other students should raise their hands but not say anything.

As a follow-up, reconvene the class and ask students to describe the use(s) of each item.

One Block, Two Blocks
Focus: non-personal
Time: 20 minutes
Materials: chalkboard and chalk; manila file folders; crayons or colored pens or pencils; exercise sheet, p. 22

Divide the class into groups of four students each. Distribute the manila file folders, crayons, and copies of the exercise sheet. Write the following directions on the board:

Go straight west.	Turn right.
Go straight east.	Turn left.
Go straight south.	Turn north.
Go straight north.	Turn south.
Turn around and go back.	Turn east.
Stop.	Turn west.
Block.	numbers 1 through 9

Instruct students to stand their file folders on the edge of their desks so that they cannot see one anothers' exercise sheets. Review the activity directions.

Explain that each student will have an opportunity to give and follow some directions. For each direction, students should use a different color crayon, pen, or pencil to keep the direction paths clear. Emphasize that students should not show their exercise sheets to one another while the exercise is in progress.

How Do I Do It?
Focus: non-personal
Time: 25 minutes
Materials: paper; pens or pencils; exercise sheets, pp. 23–24

Arrange the class in groups of three to five students each. Use the exercise sheets provided or make copies of your own preselected drawings. Distribute copies of the exercise sheets, paper, and the pens or pencils. Review the activity directions and explain to students that they each will be given an opportunity to instruct the others in their group how to draw a particular picture (p. 23 or p. 24). Students should rely primarily on oral language for their instruction, but visual clues or gestures are permissible. Stress that students should not look at anyone else's sheet while they are drawing their pictures. Have students share their pictures with one another at the end of class.

Opinions

Focus: personal
Time: 20 minutes
Materials: exercise sheets, pp. 25–26

Divide the class into groups of four to five students each. Distribute copies of the exercise sheets, one copy of both pages per group, or prepare your own "opinion" sheets. Instruct the groups to cut the exercise sheet along the dotted lines and then place the paper strips face down on one student's desk. Students take turns drawing an opinion slip from the pile, reading the question and multiple choice answers, and asking another student to select and explain his or her response. The student whose opinion was solicited becomes the next student to solicit another student's opinion.

Encourage group members to express their individual opinions on each question, to agree or disagree. A large group sharing at the end of class allows students to air their feelings about their groups' responses.

How Many Should I Take?

Focus: non-personal
Time: 15–20 minutes
Materials: small bags or bowls of candy or wrapped snacks; pairs of dice; exercise sheet, p. 28

Arrange the class in groups of three to five students. Distribute the candy or snacks, dice, and copies of the exercise sheet. Review the activity directions. Tell students that they may eat the candy/snacks when they have finished the activity. As a wrap-up, you might want to reconvene the class and have students share some of the group responses.

Cataloging

Focus: non-personal
Time: 30 minutes
Materials: magazines and catalogs with colored pictures; scissors; glue or paste; paper; pens or pencils; tape; exercise sheet, p. 27

Bring all the necessary materials to class and distribute them and copies of the exercise sheet. Review the activity directions. Explain that after students have finished gluing their pictures onto paper, you will number the pictures and display them around the room. Then each student will read his or her descriptions aloud while the others try to guess which pictures match those descriptions. Wait until each student has finished reading and the others have had time to guess before you ask the student to reveal the correct answers.

To make the guessing more difficult, have students turn over their exercise sheets and number from 1 to the last–numbered picture. Then instruct students, after each description is read, to write their guesses on their exercise sheets. Wait until all the descriptions have been read before asking students to reveal the answers.

On Focus

Directions: Look at the questions below and think about how you might answer them. Put a star (*) next to questions you like and draw a line through those you would *not* like to answer. Draw a circle around questions you might like to ask someone else.

1. What is something you really want to learn before you die?

2. Where do you think you will be five years from now?

3. How would your life be changed if there were no TV?

4. Who is someone special in your family? Why?

5. Do you want to get married someday? What is good about being married?

    What is not so good about being married?

6. What is one of the hardest things about living in the United States?

7. Who is someone you are always happy to see? Why?

8. If you found $50 in the street, what would you do with it?

9. What do you usually do on the weekends?

10. Where do you go when you need to be alone?

11. Do you enjoy sports? Do you enjoy playing or just watching? Which sports?

12. Which music do you like best—country, rock 'n' roll, or classical?

13. Whom do you miss most in your country?

14. What is the worst work you have ever done for money?

Continued

On Focus Continued

Directions: Look at the questions below and think about how you might answer them. Put a star (*) next to questions you like and draw a line through those you would *not* like to answer. Draw a circle around questions you might like to ask someone else.

1. Would you ever marry somebody from a different race or culture? Why?

2. What is something you think is scary?

3. What is something delicious?

4. What is something you have that you would hate to lose?

5. What kind of advice did your mother or father give you when you were young?

6. Who is the boss in your family?

7. What present would you like to receive?

8. Who helps you in the United States?

9. In what way do you think a religious education is important?

10. What are you saving money for?

11. What do you believe happens to a person after death?

12. How do you decide what kind of shoes to buy?

13. Why should (or shouldn't) smoking be controlled in public areas?

14. What is a bad habit you have?

The Catch-All Bag

Directions: Look at the numbered items on the table. They are all common items used in the home. Look at the list below and try to match each item with its name. Write the number of the item in the blank. If you are unsure about an item, ask another student for help. Try to guess the name of each item and its use.

_____ Number _____

_____ Number _____

_____ Number _____

_____ Number _____

_____ Number _____

_____ Number _____

_____ Number _____

_____ Number _____

_____ Number _____

_____ Number _____

_____ Number _____

_____ Number _____

_____ Number _____

_____ Number _____

_____ Number _____

One Block, Two Blocks

Directions: Look at the "map" below. Notice the little car in the bottom left corner and the boxed star in the second column near the top. Now look at the direction words and phrases on the board. Take turns giving and following the directions so that the car reaches the star. If you are giving directions, use only the words on the board. If you are following directions, use a different color crayon for each direction path. Compare your maps after each turn.

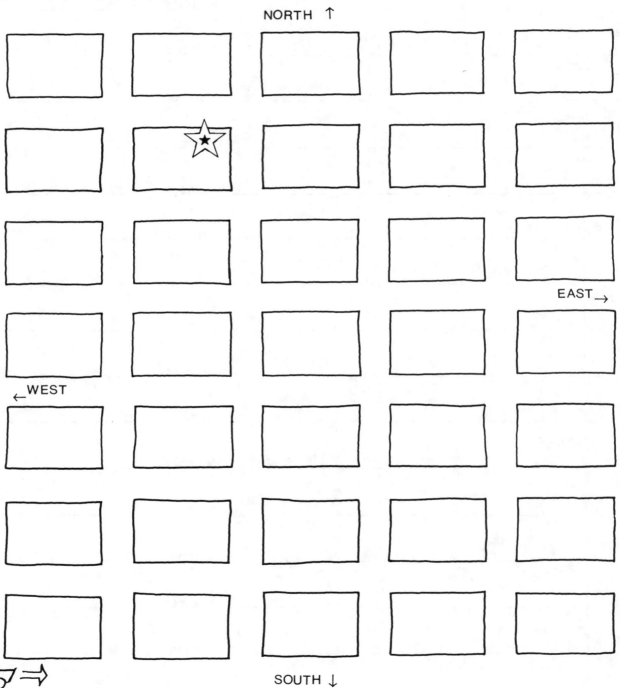

Where's My Answer?

Directions: Look at the pictures below. Choose one that you would like the others in your group to draw. Take turns telling one another how to draw the pictures. Try to draw according to one another's instructions. Do not look at anyone else's sheet!

How Do I Do It? Continued

Directions: Look at the pictures below. Choose one that you would like the others in your group to draw. Take turns telling one another how to draw the pictures. Try to draw according to one anothers' instructions. Do not look at anyone else's sheet!

1	2	3
4	5	6
7	8	9

Opinions

Directions to the teacher: Duplicate this exercise sheet and p. 26. Then follow the activity directions in the Notes to the Teacher, p. 18.

- -

1. What should you do if you get too much change at the checkout counter?

    a. Keep the money if business is good.

    b. Always keep the money if no one noticed.

    c. Return the money and point out the error.

- -

2. Should parents offer children candy?

    a. No, it will harm their teeth.

    b. Yes, it makes children happy.

    c. Sometimes, on special occasions.

- -

3. In which of these cities would you prefer to spend your vacation?

    a. San Francisco

    b. Honolulu

    c. New York

- -

4. How much spending money should a 15-year-old receive each week?

    a. $5 or less

    b. $10 to $20

    c. $20 or more

- -

Continued

---

5. Whom do you think is generally happiest? Why?

   a. married men and women

   b. single men and women

   c. married couples with children

---

6. What do you think is the best way to study?

   a. Read the textbook and take notes.

   b. Take notes in class and study the notes.

   c. Read the textbook and go to class, but don't take notes.

---

7. If someone gave you $200 in cash, what would you do with it?

   a. Give it away.

   b. Save it.

   c. Spend it.

---

8. If someone embarrassed you, what would you do?

   a. Tell the person how I feel and walk away.

   b. Try to ignore the person.

   c. Fight with the person.

Cataloging

Directions: Your teacher will bring to class some catalogs and magazines. Find colored pictures of three different people. Cut out the pictures and glue them onto three separate sheets of paper. Then, on this exercise sheet below, write a brief description of the person in each picture. Try to make your description as clear as possible so that your classmates can guess which picture you are describing.

PICTURE 1

This person's hair is _____ .

(color, style)

His or her eyes are _____ .

(color)

He or she is wearing _____ .

(clothing)

He or she looks about _____ .

(age)

This person is _____ .

(action/occupation)

PICTURE 2

This person's hair is _____ .

(color, style)

His or her eyes are _____ .

(color)

He or she is wearing _____ .

(clothing)

He or she looks about _____ .

(age)

This person is _____ .

(action/occupation)

PICTURE 3

This person's hair is _____ .

(color, style)

His or her eyes are _____ .

(color)

He or she is wearing _____ .

(clothing)

He or she looks about _____ .

(age)

This person is _____ .

(action/occupation)

How Many Should I Take?

Directions: Your teacher will bring some candy or snacks to class. Roll the dice to see how many pieces you should take. Then follow the instruction that matches the number you rolled. For example, if you rolled a 2, respond to instruction 2. and tell "one good thing about someone in the class."

For each piece of candy tell us . . .

1. one good thing about yourself.

2. one good thing about someone in the class.

3. one good thing about your teacher.

4. something you "dream" about doing in the future.

5. something you want to buy.

6. the name of a country in the world.

7. the name of a color.

9. the name of a holiday.

9. the name of an important city in the world.

10. something we eat.

11. a profession or occupation.

12. something we wear.

Strategy 3
Unified Group

Floor Map
Focus: personal
Time: 30 minutes
Materials: none

Tell students to imagine that their classroom floor is a map of the world. By way of orientation, indicate north, south, east, west and the respective locations of Asia, Africa, Europe, North and South America. Direct your students to locate their native country or city on the "map" and to stand at its approximate location. Students will have to speak to one another quite a lot to determine their relative geographical positions.

When students have located their country or city, give them a question to consider while they are standing in that place. The following are some questions we have used:

What is something special you remember about your country/city?

What circumstances caused you to leave?

Whom do you think about who still lives there?

What didn't you like about that place?

What is the most beautiful thing you have ever seen there?

After students have had some time to reflect on your question, ask three or four students to share their thoughts with the class. Then ask a second question and have three or four other students respond. Continue the activity until you have asked four or five questions and every student has had a chance to answer.

A variation of this activity is to imagine that your classroom floor is a map of the city in which you all presently live. Here are some questions to ask:

What do you find especially attractive about this place?

Who lives in your neighborhood?

What special place in your neighborhood do you visit often?

What problem do you sometimes have in your neighborhood?

Who helps you out?

After a large group sharing, you might want to divide the class into small groups to allow for more personal or extensive sharing of answers.

It's in the Bag
Focus: non-personal
Time: 30 minutes
Materials: paper bags with a different object or picture of an object in each one; paper; pens or pencils

Arrange the class in groups of four students each and give each group a paper bag containing an object or a picture of an object. Explain that each student should examine the object, discuss it with the group, and then together, in 5 to 10 minutes, write a two-sentence group description of the object. The sentences should be in the form of clues stating the object's use, features, and operation.

When each group has finished writing, choose one group to present its clues, one at a time, to the rest of the class. Students should try to guess the object's identity after each clue is read. (Only one guess per clue!) The first group continues reading its clues until the object has been identified. Continue the activity until each group has presented its clues and all objects have been correctly identified.

Here are suggestions for objects to collect or pictures to cut out: a clock, a ruler, an umbrella, a rope, a shoestring, a deck of cards, a pair of dice, a hair dryer, a slipper, vitamin pills, a can of peas, a calculator.

Mood Thermometer

Focus: personal
Time: 30 minutes
Materials: colored paper; sheets of newsprint or butcher paper (23" x 27"); colored pens or pencils; chalkboard and chalk

Introduce this activity by holding up sheets of colored paper and asking students to consider answers to such questions as, What color is happy? What color is angry? What color is jealousy? Allow students to make their own associations of colors and feelings/emotions. (There are no "right" answers.) Then ask students to think about these questions:

What color are you feeling today? Why?
What is happening that is causing you to feel that color?

While students are thinking of answers, draw the picture below on a large piece of newsprint or butcher paper.

When you have completed the drawing, invite students to select a colored pen or pencil that best represents the color they are feeling. Instruct students to write their first name only next to a point on the thermometer corresponding to the level of their present feeling (low, middle, high). When everyone has written his or her name, have students observe how graphic a presentation the "mood thermometer" is. Comment on how often we are unaware of how someone really feels unless that person tells us.

Complete the activity by having students work in small groups to finish the following sentences (written on the board):

I usually am happiest when I . . .
The thing that makes me angriest is . . .
The last time I cried was when I . . .
Sometimes I am impatient because . . .
The most frustrating thing is . . .

Picture Search

Focus: non-personal
Time: 15 minutes
Materials: complex magazine pictures; paper; pens or pencils; chalkboard and chalk

Divide the class into groups of three to five students each. Give each group one of the complex magazine pictures showing many things in the foreground and background. Distribute the paper and the pens or pencils. Allow students three minutes to identify in writing as many items in the picture as they can that begin with a certain letter of the alphabet. Each student must identify one item before another student can contribute a second one.

When the time is up, have each group pass its picture on to another group and repeat the activity using another letter of the alphabet. When each group has worked with each picture, reconvene the class for a large group sharing. Find out which group had the most items for each picture. Record that group's words on the board.

This activity offers students an excellent opportunity to increase their vocabulary and to learn from one another.

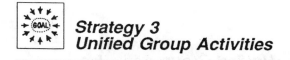
Proverbs

Focus: non-personal
Time: 30 minutes
Materials: chalkboard and chalk;
a paper bag;
exercise sheets, pp. 37–38

Use the exercise sheets provided or create your own list of proverbs, typing each half of a proverb in a separate column on a sheet of paper. Cut the paper into strips so that half of each proverb appears on a different slip. Mix the slips together in a paper bag.

Begin by defining the word *proverb* for students and writing several examples on the board. Then distribute the slips of paper so that each student has half of a complete proverb. Explain that students are to read silently what is written on their papers and then go find the student who has the second half of their proverb. They will need to circulate, questioning one another about their proverbs until they find a match. When students have found matching halves, they should sit down together and discuss the meaning of the complete proverb.

Next, have students read the proverbs aloud to the class and explain each proverb's meaning. At a later date, repeat the activity using proverbs from the students' native languages or cultures.

Puzzle It Out

Focus: non-personal
Time: 25 minutes
Materials: construction paper in 6 colors
with 5 or 6 sheets of each color;
pens or pencils; scissors or a paper
cutter; paper clips; manila file folders;
exercise sheet, p. 39

For this activity you will need to prepare ahead of time six simple puzzles from sheets of colored construction paper. Begin by assembling five or six sheets of the same color and creating a puzzle design. (Geometric or linear designs work best if you plan to use a paper cutter.) Here are some sample puzzle designs:

Cut and number the individual pieces of each puzzle (pieces of the same puzzle should have the same number) and clip them together as follows:

Repeat the procedure using six different puzzle designs and sheets of six different colors.

When you have finished cutting, numbering, and clipping all the puzzle pieces, file the puzzles—six at a time, in two different colors—in separate manila file folders, one for each group of students.

In class, arrange students in groups of six and distribute copies of the exercise sheet, one per student. Review the activity directions carefully.

As a follow-up, ask students to respond to these questions about the activity:

How did you feel about not talking?
How did you communicate with the others in your group?
How did you feel about giving?
How did you feel about taking?

The last question applies only if you decide to repeat the activity, allowing students to take the puzzle pieces they need but not to talk.

Crosswork Groups
Focus: non-personal
Time: 10 minutes
Materials: pens or pencils;
exercise sheet, p. 40

Divide the class into groups of three to five students each. Distribute copies of the exercise sheet, one per group. Explain that each group will have five minutes to write down as many different words as possible on the crosswork grid for their group. Everyone in the group must suggest one word before anyone can suggest another word. Participation from each group member is of primary importance and group members must be patient. Points will be awarded equal to the number of letters in each word. The group with the most points wins.

Here is an example of one group's crosswork grid:

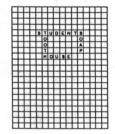

Score

students = 8
tooth = 5
house = 5
soap = 4

Total = 22 points

To facilitate the exercise and focus your students' attention, suggest a particular topic or theme with which students can associate their ideas and words. Some topics we have used are kitchen items, verbs, sports, foods, occupations, animals, Saturday night activities, cooking items, clothing items, classroom objects. For lower students, try writing a related list of words on the board from which students can choose.

Getting It All Together
Focus: non-personal
Time: 40 minutes
Materials: exercise sheets, pp. 41–42

Use the exercise sheets provided, for beginning and intermediate students, or make up your own story with a simple plot, typing each sentence of the story on a separate line of paper. Cut the story you use into individual sentence strips. Distribute the strips among the students in the class, giving each student approximately the same number.

Explain that the task is for the class to put the story back together. To do so, students will have to comprehend the content of their individual sentence strips and question one another to determine the order in which the separate parts appear. Stress that students should read and try to memorize the information on their sentence strips and avoid showing one another their strips. (To make the activity more challenging, you can collect the students' sentence strips once students have had an opportunity to memorize the content.)

Allow students 20 minutes to put the story in order. Then reconvene the class and read students the complete text. Remember that all students must participate for the activity to work.

Mystery Guest
    Focus: non-personal
    Time: 30 minutes
    Materials: exercise sheet, p. 43

This activity requires some advance planning as it involves inviting a visitor to your class. Select someone from your community or school to be your "mystery guest"—preferably someone your students haven't seen and don't know. Explain to the visitor that he or she will be expected to answer some questions from your students at the beginning of class and to return for further discussion at the end of the class period. Let your students know when the guest will be coming and what they will be doing.

Use the exercise sheet provided or make your own list of questions. Distribute copies to your students. Explain that students will have 10 minutes to question the mystery guest using the questions on their exercise sheet. Students should note the answers to their questions on the lines provided and also note which questions were not asked or answered.

When the question period is over, thank your guest and divide the class into teams of five to eight students each. Tell students that the teams are to ask each other questions about the guest from their exercise sheets. All team members must participate. If a team member answers another team's question correctly, his or her team gets a point. If the answer is incorrect, no point is given. If a team member doesn't know an answer, the other team members can help. If a team member is asked a question that the mystery guest did not answer, his or her team also receives a point. The team with the most points wins.

After 15 minutes of team questioning, invite the mystery guest back into class for five additional minutes of questions and informal discussion.

Lonely Hearts
    Focus: personal
    Time: 20 minutes
    Materials: small slips of paper; pens or pencils;
        a paper bag; tape;
        chalkboard and chalk

For this activity, your students should be well acquainted. Distribute the slips of paper and the pens or pencils and ask the students to write their names on the paper slips. Put the slips into a paper bag and have each student draw a name. (It's okay if a student draws his or her own.) Tell students that they are going to help find a wife or husband for the student whose name is on their slip of paper. They will do this by writing a Personals (Lonely Hearts, Introductions) ad for the newspaper. As an example, write this ad on the board:

I am a man, 26 years old. I am tall and very thin. I don't have much money, but I am looking for work. I am always happy and I love popular music, sports, and movies.

Instruct students to write in the first person singular and to describe their classmate's physical features, personality, interests, and other personal data. If students are unsure of their information, they can make up descriptions. Stress that the ads should be legible as well as informative.

When your students have finished writing their ads, tape them on the classroom walls and ask students to circulate, reading each ad and trying to guess who is being described. After a few minutes, reconvene the class and find out who described whom. Have students meet with their ad writer to discuss whether or not the ad was accurate and/or satisfactory.

Detectives

Focus: non-personal
Time: 30 minutes
Materials: exercise sheets, pp. 44–45

Use the exercise sheets provided and divide the class into groups, preferably of five students each. Cut the sheets into five parts and distribute them evenly so that each group has all five parts of the story.

Explain that students will have 15 minutes to work as a group, piecing the story together and solving the mystery. At the end of the time limit, reconvene the class and have the groups share their ideas *before* you reveal the solution below.

The thief had to be Mr. Spade, the insurance salesman. If the electrical power had been cut off during the robbery, he couldn't have taken the elevator down during the blackout. Elevators run on electricity. Therefore, he was lying. Detective Boris always believes that one lie leads to another.

Shadow Acting

Focus: non-personal
Time: 30 minutes
Materials: paper;
pens or pencils;
exercise sheet, p. 46

Use the exercise sheet provided, or prepare a three-frame comic strip with several characters in it. Ink out the faces of the characters so that their expressions and the situation are not readily apparent. Divide students into small groups, each one having the number of students equivalent to the number of characters in the comic strip you use. Distribute one exercise sheet per group and review the activity directions. Tell students they will have 20 minutes to create their dialogs.

When all groups have finished writing, ask for one group to volunteer to act out its dialog in front of the class.

Proverbs

Directions to the teacher: Duplicate this exercise sheet
and p. 38. Then follow the activity directions in the Notes to
the Teacher, p. 33.

Money	is the root of all evil.
A fool and his money	are soon parted.
All that glitters	is not gold.
Time	is money.
A stitch in time	saves nine.
A bird in the hand	is worth two in the bush.
A friend in need	is a friend indeed.
A watched pot	never boils.
Better late	than never.
Silence	is golden.

Continued

Two is company,	three is a crowd.
Don't cry	over spilled milk.
You can lead a horse to water	but you can't make it drink.
Necessity	is the mother of invention.
All work and no play	makes Jack a dull boy.
Don't count your chickens	before they are hatched.
Do unto others	as you would have them do unto you.
All things come	to those who wait.
Love	makes the world go around.
The way to a man's heart	is through his stomach.
Look	before you leap.

Puzzle It Out

Directions: Your group has received the pieces for six puzzles. Each puzzle, when complete, forms an $8^1/_2$" x 11" rectangle of three or four pieces. Each puzzle piece has a number written on it, and each piece is one of two colors (red or yellow, green or blue, for example). Each member of your group must complete one puzzle of one color only. To do so, follow the Steps and the Rules listed below.

Steps

1. Place all the puzzle pieces face down on a desk, a table, or the floor. Be sure that the numbers are not visible.

2. Take three or four puzzle pieces and see if they fit together.

3. If you need any different pieces or another piece, look around to see who in your group has the piece or pieces you need.

Rules

1. You may not ask anyone else for a puzzle piece or speak to anyone about your puzzle pieces.

2. You may not take any puzzle pieces from anyone in the group.

3. You may give someone else a puzzle piece and receive one from someone else.

Crosswork Groups

Directions: Work with your group to fill in the boxes below with as many words as possible. Follow the example. Everyone must suggest one word before anyone can suggest another word. Be patient and help one another by offering suggestions. Do not write in a word for someone else. Each letter of a word equals one point. The group with the most points wins.

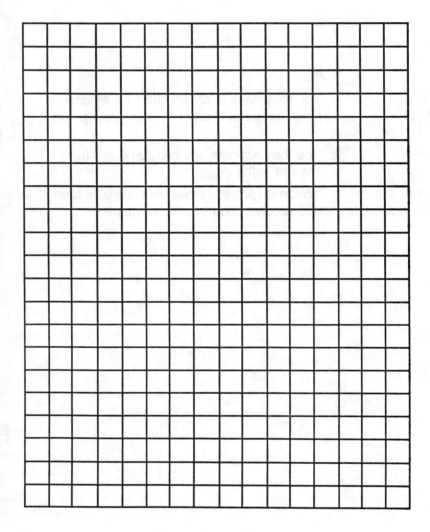

Getting It All Together

Directions to the teacher: Duplicate this exercise sheet
or p. 42 depending on the proficiency level of your students.
Then follow the activity directions in the Notes to the Teacher,
p. 34.

Story 1 (Beginning students)

A very unusual thing happened to Bill last Friday.

Although he usually works until 5:00, he stayed until 6:00 on Friday
and caught the last bus home.

On the bus, he sat by a very unusual woman.

She didn't look unusual; she just acted unusual.

During their conversation, she abruptly stood up and yelled. Bill was
embarrassed and so was the woman.

She apologized again and again, claiming she didn't know what had happened.

Bill had almost forgotten about the incident until he saw the same woman today.

She noticed Bill and ran to catch him.

She explained that she had been hypnotized at a lecture last Friday.

Every time someone said the word *wonderful*, she stood up and yelled.

Bill had apparently used the word during the conversation on the bus.

The hypnotist had forgotten to release her.

She said she was fine now.

Bill and the woman laughed and laughed.

They agreed to see each other again soon.

Continued

Story 2 (Intermediate students)

Mary and Jane usually ride to school in a car with a friend.

Yesterday they had to ride the bus.

Their friend was sick.

The bus took them on a different route.

First, it stopped at the park.

Mary loved all the flowers.

She wanted to stay and enjoy them.

Next, it stopped at the market.

Jane loves markets.

She wanted to stay and shop.

There wasn't time.

Both Jane and Mary stayed on the bus.

They really enjoyed their ride.

Now they are going to take the bus every day.

Mystery Guest

Directions: Ask your mystery guest to answer the questions below. Write your notes on the line next to each question. Circle the number of the questions that the mystery guest doesn't answer. Remember to ask each question once only.

Questions for the Mystery Guest

1. When is your birthday? _____

2. What are your favorite things to do? _____

3. What does your name mean? _____

4. Where do you work? _____

5. What is your favorite season? Why? _____

6. What is something that makes you laugh? _____

7. Have you ever won a contest? For what? _____

_____

8. What countries have you visited? _____

9. Which sports do you like to play? To watch? _____

_____

10. Who is one of your favorite people? _____

11. Where were you born? _____

12. Do you prefer to live in a big city or a small town? Why? _____

_____

Detectives

Directions to the teacher: Duplicate enough copies of this exercise sheet and p. 45 so that each student will receive one part of the complete story. Then follow the activity directions in the Notes to the Teacher, p. 36.

Part I

Mr. Benson was in his jewelry shop called Gem World at 10:30 p.m. on a Friday night. He was locking the cabinets and putting away some very expensive showpiece diamonds. These diamonds were worth $25,000 and they were displayed every Friday at Gem World.

Part II

Mr. Spade has an office above Gem World. He is an insurance salesman. He was in his office on Friday evening. He usually works late. He claimed he was there when the lights went out.

Part III

The janitor, Mr. Johnson, confirmed that the electricity went off at 10:30 p.m. He tried to find the fuse box to turn the lights back on, but he was knocked down by someone else in the building. He heard Mr. Benson call to him right after the lights went out. After the janitor got back to his feet, it took him about 10 minutes to get the lights back on.

Continued

Part IV

When Mr. Johnson finally got back to Gem World, he found Mr. Benson lying on the floor. It took him several minutes to revive him. He had been knocked out. The diamonds had been stolen. Mr. Johnson called the police. Before the police arrived, Mr. Spade, the insurance agent, appeared on the scene. He said he was surprised to find Mr. Benson had been knocked out. He said he had taken the elevator down when he heard Mr. Benson calling the janitor.

Part V

The policeman in charge of the investigation was Detective Boris. He listened to the entire story and then arrested Mr. Spade. The diamonds were later found hidden in his office. How did Detective Boris solve the case? What was the clue?

Look Who's Talking! ©1995 by Alta Book Center Publishers
Permission is granted to reproduce this page for classroom use.

Shadow Acting

Directions: This comic strip has several characters in it. You cannot see their faces. With your group, decide what is going on in the comic strip and write a dialog or conversation for it. Each one of you should take the part of one character. You will be given an opportunity to present your dialog to the rest of the class.

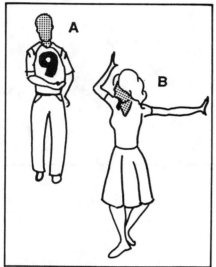  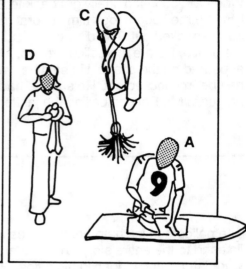

A _____

B _____

A _____

B _____

A _____

B _____

A _____

B _____

A _____

C _____

D _____

A _____

C _____

D _____

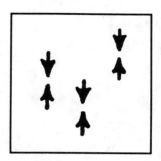

Strategy 4
Dyad

Blind Faith

Focus: non-personal
Time: 30 minutes
Materials: blindfolds; sets of instructions;
pens or pencils;
exercise sheet, p. 53

Divide the class into student pairs. Explain that each student will have a chance to be blindfolded and led by his or her partner according to a specific set of instructions. While students are being led, they should hold hands or link arms and pay attention to their feelings and sensations.

Demonstrate how to tie a blindfold correctly so that a person cannot see, and give each student a set of leading instructions marked A or B (see examples below). The instructions should reflect the location of your classroom and the floor plan of your school.

Example A

Lead your partner out of the classroom. Turn right. Go up the stairs to the second floor. Turn your partner around five or six times. Follow the upstairs hall west. Return to the first floor by the back stairs. Lead your partner back to the class.

Example B

Lead your partner out of the classroom. Turn left outside the door. Follow the hall south and turn right at the end. Stop. Turn your partner around five or six times. Go back along the same hall and return to the classroom.

When each student has had an opportunity to be blindfolded and to lead another student, divide the class into new student pairs and distribute copies of the exercise sheet. Give partners five minutes each to question one another and then reconvene the class for a question-and-answer session using the exercise sheet.

Who, What, When, Where, and Why?

Focus: non-personal
Time: 30 minutes
Materials: pens or pencils;
exercise sheet, p. 54

Arrange the class in student pairs and distribute copies of the exercise sheet, one sheet per pair. Review the activity directions. When students have finished writing, ask different pairs to share their ideas with the class for about 10 minutes. Encourage discussion of contrasts and similarities and the reasons why our visual perceptions often differ.

5" x 7" Focus

Focus: personal
Time: 30–40 minutes
Materials: 5" x 7" index cards;
pens or pencils

Distribute the index cards and the pens or pencils. Explain that students are to write words or phrases in answer to questions you will ask. Stress that complete answers are unnecessary; only enough information should be noted to remind students of the questions and their ideas or answers.

After student have finished taking notes, have them work with a partner, sharing answers. Partners should decide who will begin and which answers they want to share. Some questions may seem unanswerable or too personal for some students. Set a time limit and signal students at the halfway point so that both partners get a chance to speak.

The sample questions below focus on individual or group values, such as religion, politics, family, romance, work, leisure, and so on.

Who is very special to you in your family?
What was your first job?
What are things that you like about this city?
What are three things that you can do very well?
What book has influenced your life?
How is religion important in your life?
How do you spend most of your money?
What do you like to do when you are alone?
How would you like to change your life?
What place do you hope to visit someday?
What is something you want but can't afford?
What are you afraid of?
Who is someone you admire?
How do you spend your Saturday nights?
What is a food that you just can't eat?

Comic Strip

Focus: non-personal
Time: 20 minutes
Materials: pens or pencils;
exercise sheet, p. 55

Divide the class into student pairs. Distribute copies of the exercise sheet or prepare your own two-character three- or four-frame comic strip from which the dialog has been removed. Review the activity directions. Then allow 15 minutes for each pair to write a dialog. When everyone has finished writing, ask different pairs to read their dialogs to the class.

Distance and Space

    Focus: personal
     Time: 15 minutes
Materials: pens or pencils;
           exercise sheet, p. 56

Divide the class into student pairs and have the partners stand on opposite sides of the classroom facing one another. Distribute copies of the exercise sheet, one per student. Instruct students to ask each other the first three questions on the sheet and to write the answers on the lines provided. When everyone has had an opportunity to answer the questions, stop and ask students to ask/respond to some of the questions aloud. Find out how students feel talking to someone at such a distance.

Instruct students to step about four feet closer to their partner and to ask the next three questions. When each partner has had a chance to answer, have the students stop. Find out how they feel talking to one another at this closer distance.

Now ask your students to start walking slowly toward one another until they are approximately three inches away. Find out how they feel talking at this distance. (Most students will feel uncomfortable.) Have students back up until they feel at a comfortable distance for carrying on a conversation. Then ask them to reflect on answers to the following questions:

Is everyone in the room standing at the same distance from their partner? Is your partner standing at a distance that is comfortable for you?

What is the distance at which you feel most comfortable talking to someone? (That distance is called your "personal space.")

Do you stand closer to people you know better than to those who are strangers?

How close do you think Americans generally stand to one another?

We've Got Class

    Focus: non-personal
     Time: 20 minutes
Materials: chalkboard and chalk;
           paper; pens or pencils

Divide the class into student pairs and write the following classification headings on the board (or choose your own): Decorations, Breakfast Foods, Things That Fold, Things That Break Easily, and Electrical Items. Ask students to think of as many different items as possible that can be classified under these headings. One student only should write down the pair's ideas. Allow time for a large group sharing of answers at the end of class. The pair with the greatest number of accurate items wins.

Where Do I Put It?

    Focus: non-personal
     Time: 20 minutes
Materials: manila file folders;
           paper; pens or pencils;
           exercise sheets, pp. 57–58

Have students work in pairs, sitting opposite one another with a manila file folder standing between them. The students should be able to hear and see each other but be unable to view each other's paper or materials.

Distribute copies of the two exercise sheets. Each partner should receive a different sheet. Explain that students with the illustrated sheet (p. 57) must explain to their partner how and where to draw the various illustrations on the blank grid (p. 58). Have students change roles and repeat the exercise, using clean copies of the blank grid and the same picture grid, or one that you have prepared.

You can vary this activity by preparing and distributing a list of 10 to 20 nouns to each student in a pair. Students take turns selecting a noun and telling their partner where to draw a representative picture on their blank grids. Both students should draw the picture, then compare their drawings. Good nouns for the list are hammer, comb, snake, spoon, lamp, pen, cup, tree, and so on. Minimal pairs that are easy to draw (for example, ship-sheep, map-mop), can also be used. Each student draws a picture for one word of the pair.

What Can You Do with This?

    Focus: non-personal
     Time: 20 minutes
Materials: chalkboard and chalk;
           10 common objects;
           paper; pens or pencils

For this activity you will need to collect and bring to class 10 common objects. Place the objects on a table or desk in the classroom. Divide the class into student pairs and have each pair select five objects to work with. Students should brainstorm at least 10 different uses for each of the objects. For example, a rope can (1) tie someone up, (2) be a belt, (3) tow a car, (4) be a fishing line, (5) keep a door shut, and so on. One student only should write down the pair's ideas. Circulate among the pairs to answer any questions. After 10 minutes, follow up with a large group sharing of ideas. Record the ideas on the board for everyone to see.

Here are some suggestions for common objects: a soda-pop bottle, an umbrella, an eraser, a pencil, a bucket, a rope, a box, a can opener, a book, a sock, a coffee mug, a spoon, a shoe, a broken watch.

**Strategy 4
Dyad Activities**

This Week

> Focus: personal
> Time: 20–30 minutes
> Materials: paper; pens or pencils

Divide the class into student pairs and distribute the paper and the pens or pencils. Ask students to draw a large circle, label it This Week and divide it into four sections. Then have students write answers, one in each of the circle's quadrants, to these questions:

> What decision have you made this week?
> What have you done to make someone happy this week?
> What small (or great) success have you had this week?
> What compliment have you received this week?

When students have finished writing, have them share two of their answers with their partner. Then have students change partners and share their other two answers with that person. Continue until all students have shared all their answers with the rest of the class.

Life Cycle

> Focus: personal
> Time: 30 minutes
> Materials: chalkboard and chalk;
> pens or pencils; crayons or colored
> pens or pencils; exercise sheet, p. 59

Divide the class into student pairs and distribute copies of the exercise sheet. Review the activity directions and answer any questions. You may want to duplicate copies of the sample life cycle chart below or draw a similar model on the board.

Orange	I came to the United States
Red	
	I had my first baby
Blue	I got married
Green	I got my braces off
Yellow	
	I started school
Pink	My brother was born
Purple	My birth

Word Associations

> Focus: non-personal
> Time: 25 minutes
> Materials: paper; pens or pencils

For this activity you will need to prepare a list of 10 to 15 stimulus words. Divide the class into student pairs and distribute the paper and the pens or pencils. Tell the class that you are going to read aloud a list of words, one by one. Students should write down each word and the first word (or phrase) that comes to mind in response to your stimulus word; for example, if you read *cat*, students might think/write *mouse*. Emphasize that there are no correct answers. The purpose of the activity is to demonstrate how words trigger different associations and responses in different people.

When the students have finished writing, have them, in pairs, share their responses with each other. Then, in a large group, discuss how meanings and associations come from experience and instruction, and how misunderstandings and miscommunication occur when people do not share the same experiences or teachings. Brainstorm ways to assure understanding by and of others.

Personality Partners

> Focus: personal
> Time: 15 minutes
> Materials: pens or pencils;
> exercise sheet, p. 60

Divide the class into student pairs and distribute copies of the exercise sheet. Then read the following directions out loud:

- Under the word ME, write five words or phrases that make you special, that describe you.
- Under the words MY PARTNER, write five things that you feel describe your partner.
- Exchange descriptions with your partner. Compare your self-description with what your partner wrote about you.

Allow enough time between directions for students to complete each task. Then ask students to answer the questions on their exercise sheets.

Back to Back
Focus: personal
Time: 15 minutes
Materials: pens or pencils;
exercise sheets, pp. 61–64

Divide the class into student pairs and have the students sit back to back at their desks. Distribute copies of the A exercise sheets so that each partner receives a different sheet (A–1 or A–2). Explain that students will have 10 minutes each to ask their partners the questions on their sheets and to take notes on answers.

When students have finished asking their questions, have them form a circle to discuss their answers. Encourage comment on how students felt being unable to face their partner while talking. Focus on some of the obvious advantages of face-to-face communication (facial expressions, gestures, and so on) and find out whether students had to repeat their questions or answers often. Explore the possible reasons for communication difficulties.

Have students meet with their partners again, this time for face-to-face interviews. Use the B set of questions or redistribute clean copies of the A questions, making sure that each student receives the alternate set. Allow time for follow-up discussion.

Creative Grids
Focus: non-personal
Time: 30 minutes
Materials: manila file folders (optional);
scissors; exercise sheets, pp. 65–66

Divide the class into student pairs and distribute copies of the exercise sheets. Instruct students to cut p. 65 into 12 individual picture squares (or, to save class time, prepare the squares ahead of class). Have students sit back to back or with a manila file folder standing between them so that they are unable to see each other's paper or materials.

Tell students that they must place their pictures on their blank grids (p. 66) in exactly the same order, without showing one another their grids. Have one student be the speaker and the other the listener. The speaker describes the pictures and tells the listener where to place them. When all the picture squares are in place, have students compare their grids. Repeat the exercise with partners switching speaker/listener roles.

This exercise can also be done using sets of 9 different shapes cut from tagboard. If students experience difficulty in describing the shapes, teach them the phrase, It looks like a(n) _____ .

It's Your Choice
Focus: personal
Time: 15 minutes
Materials: pens or pencils;
exercise sheets, pp. 67–68

Divide the class into student pairs. Distribute copies of the first exercise sheet, p. 67, or make your own multiple-choice exercise. (If you prepare your own, you might prefer to select activities related to a particular topic, such as school, work, leisure, family, or else based on a specific grammatical structure, such as *I wish I could/knew/worked/understood/had . . . .*) Review the activity directions.

When students have finished discussing their choices, have them repeat the activity with a new partner and/or use the second exercise sheet, p. 68. As a follow-up, ask students to write a short composition on one of the topics.

Charting the Way
Focus: non-personal
Time: 45 minutes
Materials: pens or pencils;
exercise sheets, pp. 69–72

Divide the class into student pairs and distribute copies of the exercise sheets, A–1, A–2, or B–1, B–2, a different copy for each partner. Explain that students are to ask their partner for the information that is missing from their own charts. They are to write that information in the empty chart boxes. When the charts are complete, partners should work together to answer the questions below the charts. If students have different answers, they need to review their information to determine where a mistake occurred.

Blind Faith

Directions: Ask your partner the questions below.
Write his or her answers on the lines provided.
Share your answers with the class.

1. Do you like to be in the dark? Why or why not? _____

2. How did you feel when your partner put on your blindfold? _____

3. How did you feel when your partner turned you around? _____

4. How did you feel toward your partner while he or she was leading you? _____

   _____

5. Was it hard to trust him/her? Why? _____

   _____

6 Was your partner careful? _____

   _____

7. Did your partner do things that frightened you? _____

8. Did you do things that frightened your partner? _____

9. Did your partner go too slowly or too fast? _____

10. Did you get mixed up?_____

11. Was the blindfold placed so that you couldn't see? _____

12. Did you talk during this activity? If so, what did you say? _____

Who, What, When, Where, and Why?

Directions: With your partner, look at the pictures below and complete the sentences following each one.

His name is —————————————————

He's carrying a bag ———————————————

Inside the bag is ——————————————

He's going ———————————————————

because ———————————————————————

His name is —————————————————

He's carrying a large box ———————————

Inside the box is ——————————————

He's going ———————————————————

because ———————————————————————

Her name is —————————————————

She's carrying a basket ————————————

Inside the basket is ————————————

She's going ———————————————————

because ———————————————————————

Comic Strip

Directions: With your partner, look at the comic strip below. Decide what the characters might be saying to one another. Take turns writing in the dialog and be prepared to read your dialog aloud to the class.

Distance and Space

Directions: Ask your partner the questions below and write
his or her answers on the lines provided.

1. What is your address? _____

_____

2. What kind of things do you like to do in your English class? _____

_____

3. With whom do you live now? _____

_____

4. Where do you usually shop for groceries? How often do you shop? _____

_____

5. What would you do if you won the state lottery for $2 million? _____

_____

_____

6. What is your idea of a "dream job"? What kind of work would you really love to do? _____

_____

_____

Where Do I Put It?

Directions to the teacher: Read the activity directions in
the Notes to the Teacher, p. 50; then duplicate the number of
copies you need of this exercise sheet and p. 58.

Continued

Where Do I Put It! Continued

Directions to the teacher: Read the activity directions in the Notes to the Teacher, p. 50; then duplicate the number of copies you need of this exercise sheet and p. 57.

1	2	3
4	5	6
7	8	9

Life Cycle

Directions: Identify the six most important events in your life so far. Then look at the life cycle chart below. Write your age at the top of the chart and record your six events on the chart. Label each event and color each one a different color. When you have completed your chart, share the information with your partner and ask each other the following questions:

1. How old were you when the first event occurred? _____

2. Which events occurred together? _____

3. Did you choose your colors for any particular reason? _____

4. Which event was the most recent? _____

5. Which event do you remember better than the others? _____

6. How is your chart similar to or different from mine? _____

7. Which event would you like to repeat? _____

8. Which event is the most important to you? _____

My age is _____ .

Personality Partners

Directions: Follow the directions your teacher reads to you.
Then discuss the questions below with your partner.

ME	MY PARTNER
1. _____	1. _____
2. _____	2. _____
3. _____	3. _____
4. _____	4. _____
5. _____	5. _____

Questions

1. What surprises did you find?

2. What things did your partner write about you that you didn't mention?

3. What did you write about your partner that he or she didn't mention?

4. What did you learn about how someone else sees you?

5. Did you look for the same things in your partner that you looked for in yourself?

Back to Back

Directions to the teacher: Duplicate copies of this exercise sheet and pp. 62–64. Then follow the activity directions in the Notes to the Teacher, p. 52.

Questions A-1

1. If you are not studying in the evening, what do you like to do?

   _____

2. What is the most difficult part of your day?

   _____

3. Who makes you happy? Why?

   _____

4. Who is your most favorite TV star?

   _____

5. Do you smoke? If yes, how long have you been a smoker?

   _____

6. How many brothers and sisters do you have? Who is your favorite brother or sister? Why?

   _____

7. How long have you been in the United States?

   _____

8. Have you lived in any other American cities?

   _____

Continued

Back to Back Continued

Directions to the teacher: Duplicate copies of this exercise sheet and pp. 61, 63-64. Then follow the activity directions in the Notes to the Teacher, p. 52.

Questions A–2

1. Are you a morning person or a night person?

   _____

2. What time of the day do you like most? Why?

   _____

3. Do you smoke? Does it bother you if people smoke right next to you indoors?

   _____

4. What food is very common for people in your country?

   _____

5. What color do you like to wear?

   _____

6. Do you have a pair of tennis or running shoes? What kind? What color?

   _____

7. Do you ride a bicycle? If yes, what kind of bicycle is it?

   _____

8. How long do you plan to stay here in the United States?

   _____

Continued

Back to Back Continued

Directions to the teacher: Duplicate copies of this exercise sheet and pp. 61–62, 64. Then follow the activity directions in the Notes to the Teacher, p. 52.

Questions B–1

1. Where were you born?

_____

2. What is your native language?

_____

3. Do you speak any other languages?

_____

4. How long have you been in this city?

_____

5. Where do you live now?

_____

6. What is your favorite American food?

_____

7. What TV show do you hate to miss?

_____

8. Are you married or single? Which would you prefer to be?

_____

Continued

Back to Back Continued

Directions to the teacher: Duplicate copies of this exercise sheet and pp. 61–63. Then follow the activity directions in the Notes to the Teacher, p. 52.

Questions B–2

1. Can you drive a car? What kind of car would you like to own?

   _____

2. Who is your favorite movie actress or actor?

   _____

3. What is the biggest problem you have with learning English?

   _____

4. What is something about American people that is different from people in your country?

   _____

5. Do you like to go to bed early or to stay up late?

   _____

6. Do you receive many letters from home? Who are they from?

   _____

7. Do you have a watch? What kind? Where did you get it?

   _____

8. Where do you shop for food?

   _____

Creative Grids

Directions to the teacher: Duplicate two copies each of
this exercise sheet. Then follow the activity directions in the
Notes to the Teacher, p. 52.

Continued

Creative Grids Continued

Directions to the teacher: Duplicate two copies each of this exercise sheet. Then follow the activity directions in the Notes to the Teacher, p. 52.

It's Your Choice

Directions: Read the questions below and circle the answer—a, b, or c— that best describes how you feel. Then share your answers with your partner and explain why you chose the answers you did.

1. Which household chore do you prefer to do?

   a. Wash the dishes.

   b. Iron the shirts.

   c. Clean the bathroom.

2. Where would you like to be on a Saturday afternoon?

   a. In the mountains with a friend.

   b. Sleeping in the sun in the backyard.

   c. At a discount store with $100.

3. Where would you prefer to live?

   a. In a cabin in the mountains.

   b. In a big city.

   c. In a small town.

4. Which would you least like to do?

   a. Listen to a classical music concert.

   b. Listen to a political speech.

   c. Listen to cars honking their horns.

5. Which is the most difficult?

   a. Finding a boyfriend or girlfriend.

   b. Speaking English.

   c. Paying my bills.

Continued

It's Your Choice Continued

Directions: Read the questions below and circle the answer—a, b, or c—that best describes how you feel. Then share your answers with your partner and explain why you chose the answers you did.

1. What do you need more of?

   a. Free time.

   b. Money.

   c. Exercise.

2. When do you have the most fun?

   a. When I'm alone.

   b. When I'm with one or two friends.

   c. When I'm with a lot of people.

3. What kind of work would you prefer to do?

   a. Hard and dirty work for $700 a week.

   b. Clean and easy work for $300 a week.

   c. Fun, entertaining work for $200 a week.

4. What kind of person are you?

   a. Someone who looks for the good in everything.

   b. Someone who looks for bargains in the stores.

   c. Someone who looks for excitement.

5. What is important to you?

   a. To love others.

   b. To understand myself very well.

   c. To work hard for my future.

Look Who's Talking! ©1995 by Alta Book Center Publishers
Permission is granted to reproduce this page for classroom use.

Charting the Way

Directions to the teacher: Duplicate this exercise sheet and pp. 70–74. Then follow the activity directions in the Notes to the Teacher, p. 52.

	Utah		Arizona	
	82,096		113,417	
Population of the State		2,850,000	1,250,000	1,303,302
Largest City	Salt Lake City		Phoenix	
		Snow Skiing		Carlsbad Caverns Chaco Canyon Indian ruins

Questions A–1

Work with your partner to answer these questions.

1. Which state is the largest? _____

2. Which two states are closest in size? _____

3. Which state has the biggest city? What is the name of the city? _____

4. Which two states have similar tourist attractions? _____

5. What is Arizona's largest city? _____

6. Why do most people visit Colorado? _____

7. Where is Chaco Canyon? _____

8. Which two states have the greatest difference in population? _____

_____

Continued

Charting the Way Continued

Directions to the teacher: Duplicate this exercise sheet and pp. 69, 71–72. Then follow the activity directions in the Notes to the Teacher, p. 52.

	Colorado		New Mexico
Size in Square Miles	103,766		121,421
	1,307,500	2,450,000	
	Denver		Albuquerque
Major Tourist Attraction	Snow Skiing Temple Square	Grand Canyon warm, sunny climate	

Questions A–2

Work with your partner to answer these questions.

1. Which state is the largest? _____

2. Which two states are the closest in size? _____

3. Which state has the biggest city? What is the name of the city? _____

4. Which two states have similar tourist attractions? _____

5. What is Arizona's largest city? _____

6. Why do most people visit Colorado? _____

7. Where is Chaco Canyon? _____

8. Which two states have the greatest difference in population? _____

Continued

Charting the Way Continued

Directions to the teacher: Duplicate this exercise sheet and pp. 69–70, 72. Then follow the activity directions in the Notes to the Teacher, p. 52.

Student		Major	Languages Spoken	
John Williams		English Literature		Guitar Racketball
Yukiko Sato	Japan		Japanese English	
	United States	Physical Education		
			Arabic English French	Soccer Swimming
Karen Wright	Great Britain	French		Calligraphy Water Color Painting
Anna Goiri			French, Spanish, Italian, German, English	
Punsak Lertananubal	Thailand	Business Administration		Basketball, Swimming, Badminton

Questions B–1

Work with your partner to answer these questions.

1. How many students speak French? _____

2. How many languages are spoken by the seven students? _____

3. Which three students have similar hobbies? _____

4. What is origami? _____

5. What is calligraphy? _____

6. Which students play stringed instruments? _____

7. Which student is probably an artist? _____

8. Which language is spoken by all the students? _____

9. Which student is from the Middle East? _____

10. Which student is from Latin America? _____

Continued

Charting the Way Continued

Directions to the teacher: Duplicate this exercise sheet and pp. 69–71. Then follow the activity directions in the Notes to the Teacher, p. 52.

	Country			Hobbies
	Canada		French, English, Spanish	
		Computer Science		Tennis, Origami
Andrew Marks			German, English	Violin, Reading Westerns
Davood Ahmed	Jordan	Civil Engineering		
			Spanish, English, Portuguese	
	Venezuela	Marketing		Soccer Science Fiction
			Thai French English	

Questions B–2

Work with your partner to answer these questions.

1. How many students speak French?_____

2. How many languages are spoken by the seven students? _____

3. Which three students have similar hobbies?_____

4. What is origami? _____

5. What is calligraphy? _____

6. Which students play stringed instruments? _____

7. Which student is probably an artist? _____

8. Which language is spoken by all the students? _____

9. Which student is from the Middle East? _____

10. Which student is from Latin America? _____

Strategy 5
Small Group

Controversy

Focus: personal
Time: 15 minutes
Materials: chalkboard and chalk

Before beginning class, write a controversial statement in big letters on the board. (Some sample statements are given below.) Make sure that the statement can be seen by students sitting in the back of the room. Say nothing to students about what you have written.

About 20 minutes before class ends, ask students to form groups of three or four students each. Explain that you would like each student to "take a stand" on the statement you have written. Students must agree or disagree with the statement and explain why. After the first student in each group has commented, a second student must repeat or restate exactly what the first student said, to the first student's satisfaction. If the first student is unhappy with the restatement, he or she may ask the second student to repeat the restatement until it has been clearly presented and understood. Then, the first student's statement is commented on by the second student, and a third student restates the second student's comment. The activity continues until everyone in the group has had a chance to comment and to restate.

Here are some statements that we have used successfully. Use them or write your own statements to correspond with your students' interests or with current events:

Immigration to the United States should be open and unlimited.

People who marry should stay married. There should be no divorce.

All drunk drivers should be sent to prison.

Parents should allow their teenage children to choose their own hair and clothing styles.

TV is a total waste of time. It makes people stupid.

High school cafeterias should not be allowed to sell junk food.

National pride is ridiculous. All borders and boundaries should be abolished.

Cigarettes and cigars should be banned. They cause cancer.

Possessions

Focus: personal
Time: 15 minutes
Materials: chalkboard and chalk

Have the class form groups of six students each. Explain that the groups will be given an opportunity to talk about things that are precious or important to them, things they need or would hate to lose. Choose one of the following topics (or create your own), write it on the board, and have students take turns sharing answers in their groups:

- Something that I always carry with me is . . .
- Something that is very important to me is . . .
- Something that my mother gave me is . . .
- Something that I forgot to pack when I came to the United States is . . .
- Something that I just bought is . . .
- Something that makes me feel peaceful is . . .
- Something that I use all the time is . . .
- Something that makes me feel happy is . . .
- Something that brings back memories is . . .
- Something that I would not lend to a friend is . . .

Guided Fantasies
Focus: personal
Time: 15 minutes
Materials: none

Have students sit in small groups of three or four students each. Tell them that you are going to read aloud a fantasy (an imagined story) that they will be asked to complete. Instruct students to sit comfortably and relax. They may close their eyes if they wish.

Read one of the fantasies below, slowly, in a soft, clear voice. Use appropriate intonation to make the story seem real. You may want to add (or delete) details to make the story more comprehensible and interesting to your students.

Allow students two or three minutes to discover their own personal endings to the fantasy. Then have students share their ideas within their groups. No one is required to share; some students may prefer to listen and comment only or to write their ideas down on paper. All options are acceptable.

Fantasy 1 — A Message
It is a beautiful sunny Saturday morning in "*city or town*". You are sitting outside in the front yard of your home, relaxing in the sunshine and drinking your favorite early morning drink. The neighborhood is quiet. You look at the other houses on your street, the trees, the fences. You see the same dog that is always running around.

Then you notice a man on a bicycle coming down the street. He is wearing a green uniform and carrying a bag. He seems to be coming to your house. Yes, he sure is. You watch as he approaches your house. He stops his bicycle and gets off and walks up to you, calling your name. You say to him "That's me!" He says that he is from Express Union telegraph service and that he has a very exciting telegram for you. He smiles and says how much he loves to deliver good news! He hands you the telegram with a wink and another smile. He says, "Sign here, please."

You sign his paper and look over the yellow envelope. The delivery man rides off down the street on his bicycle. What can this be? Who is it from? Good news? You tear open the envelope and read the message. Your hands are shaking with excitement as you read the good news. You were sure hoping to get this news! Read over the telegram, then share the message with your group.

Fantasy 2 — The Gift Box
It is the end of the day. You have been very busy all day—running, thinking, working, hurrying. You're feeling a little tired, but it was a good day—satisfying and productive. You approach your house. You're really glad to be there where it is warm and comfortable and familiar. You reach for the doorknob and look for your key. Where is it? Oh, here it is. You discover suddenly that the door is already unlocked! That's strange. You recall locking it this morning. You always lock it!

You walk in. Everything looks the same, smells the same. Everything appears to be just as you left it. You take off your old jacket and throw it on the sofa. As you walk into the kitchen, you notice a package on the table. A package? That's strange! It's all wrapped up like a present. What is this? What size is the package? Very small? Very big? Look at the color of the paper. Notice the ribbon on top and the little note with your name on it. How curious! What could it be? Who could it be from? You sit down at the table, running your hands over the paper; you're not sure that you want to open this package. Oh well, go ahead. It's for you!

You read the little note. It says, "Inside is a gift that you really want right now!" You slowly and carefully tear off the paper and the ribbon. You open the box and look inside. Wow! Look at that! That's wonderful! You are totally surprised. And look who it is from! How nice! Look over the gift and read the card again, then describe what you found in the box to your group.

Continued

Fantasy 3 — Magic Vitamins

You're feeling kind of blah. Not sick, but not really well. Not sad, but not really happy. Not lazy, but not full of energy either. You're not really lonely, but it might be nice if someone visited you once in a while! You're just kind of in the middle. Your life isn't perfect now, but it isn't too bad. There are just a few things you would like to change, that's all. So, you decide to look for some help.

You put on your jacket, open your door, leave your house, and start walking. You walk and walk with nowhere special in mind. After a while, you find yourself on a street you never walked down before. You look into all sorts of different store windows. Something in a little shop catches your eye. You stop and look at the display in the window—vitamins—all kinds of vitamins. Vitamins you have never seen before, Vitamin HK, Vitamin Z, Vitamin X! What can these be for?

You walk into the shop and pick up one bottle of each vitamin—HK, X, and Z. You take them to the clerk and put them on the counter. "What are these vitamins for?" you ask him. "What do they do?" He tells you they are special vitamins. Each one will change your life in some way, some good way. He asks you for $3.00.

You take your bottles of vitamins home and swallow one vitamin from each bottle. By 6 o'clock that evening all three pills are starting to take effect. You are starting to feel really different, really happy with the changes that are beginning to happen in your life. These are truly wonderful vitamins. Experience these changes for awhile, then tell your group what effect they are having on your life.

Fantasy 4 — The Perfect Machine

On your kitchen table are various tools—a hammer, screwdriver and screws, bolts, nuts, wire, wire cutters. On the table is a set of plans too. You have worked and worked and finally have finished building your marvelous machine! Look it over. It is truly a fine invention. On the top you have put a small red button. On the back is a little silver wheel. On the right side you have added a lever that reads Pull Me. In front there is a big crank. This is a very special little machine. You invented it. There is nothing like it in the whole world.

Describe your machine to the others in your group and tell them what happens when you flip the switch, push the button, turn the wheel, wind the crank, and pull the lever.

Fantasy 5 — The Big Win

You are lying on your bed. It is not very comfortable; it feels hard and lumpy. You can't sleep. You're too cold. No, you're too hot. Throw off the blankets. No, pull them back up. You hear traffic noises outside your window. You turn over again and again. The room is very dark. You wish you had someone to talk to. You have a hundred problems running through your head.

Suddenly, in the middle of this terrible night, the telephone rings. You reach out in the darkness trying to find the telephone. Oops! You dropped the receiver on the floor. Where is it? Oh, here it is. "Hello?" A man's voice says, "Congratulations! This is the Big Win Show on TV. You have just won an all expenses-paid holiday anywhere in the world! Starting tomorrow at 8 o'clock in the morning, you will be with any person you choose in any country or city you choose. You can stay for two days and do anything you like!" You have to decide in one minute where and with whom you would like to be.

Think about your good luck and then share with your group how, where, and with whom you will spend your ideal 48 hours.

Continued

Fantasy 6 — The Wise Man

You are walking along a quiet beach. It is a cool, gray day. You breathe in the salt air and walk and walk and walk, watching the waves roll in and out. You have never been on this long, deserted beach before. You don't see any other people around. And that feels okay with you; you need time to be alone to just think about life. You listen to the singing of the sea birds and notice them flying across the very tops of the waves. You feel the sand collecting in your shoes. You finally come to a place where the rocks reach to the water's edge and you have to wait for a wave to go out before you can run around to the other side. As the wave moves slowly back, you quickly run around the big rocks and continue to walk down the beach.

Suddenly, you notice up ahead a dark opening in the wall of the cliff that towers along one side of the beach. You walk slowly toward it and peek inside. It is very dark and it looks like a big, black room, big enough to stand up in! You are curious. You slowly step inside and look deep into the darkness. You carefully walk deeper and deeper into the dark cave. Running your hands along the cool, damp wall, you try very hard not to fall in the blackness.

You continue to walk slowly and carefully into the cave for a few more minutes. Funny, but you almost detect the smell of flowers . . . roses, maybe? That's strange. The wall takes a turn to the left, and as you round the corner, you see a faint pink light glowing somewhere up ahead of you. A light? What can that be? Are you nervous in here? No . . . you feel fine. You feel very curious and decide to keep walking toward the little light and the smell of roses.

You step slowly and quietly and the light becomes brighter and clearer. You continue forward and then you feel the cave take another slight turn to the left. As you feel your way around another turn, you find yourself face to face with an old, old man who is sitting on a large, flat rock. His face is friendly and peaceful. His hair is long and pinkish white. The light almost seems to be coming from his hair and body! He looks at you very calmly with a little smile—it seems as if he has been waiting for you. His eyes look directly into your eyes, and when he speaks, his voice is as soft as a cloud.

"Have you come for your answer? I know you have come to me with a question."

You look at his face and you know that he really could answer any question you might have. You know that he would be correct. There has been a very important question on your mind lately. You know that. Maybe you could ask this old man and he could help you. He is patient. He smiles and waits for you to speak. Go ahead, ask him now and listen carefully to his wise answer. Consider what it means to you.

Tell your group what the question was that you asked this old man and what answer he gave to you.

Picture Solving

Focus: non-personal
Time: 30 minutes
Materials: mounted magazine pictures; paper; pens or pencils; 3" x 5" index cards;

Ahead of class, mount magazine pictures on construction paper and number them, allowing for two pictures per student. Divide the class into groups of three to five students each and distribute the pictures. Ask each group to appoint a secretary to write down five specific questions that the group has about each picture.

Choose one group to hold up its pictures in numerical sequence (or line the pictures up on the chalk tray) so that everyone in the class can see them. Then have each student in the group read a question for the rest of the class to answer. The class must first decide which picture the question is about and then what the answer to that question is. If the questions are not specific enough, individual students can suggest changes in the questions that would make them relate more closely to the pictures.

As a follow–up, have students make question cards for each picture. Mix the cards and pictures together and give one card or picture to each student. Have students try to match cards and pictures by questioning one another without revealing either their card or picture. Finish with some large group work focusing on the following (or similar) questions:

What questions could have been asked about more than one picture?
What questions did you have a hard time answering?
Did you have a favorite picture? Why or why not?
How did your group work together?
Did anyone talk too much?
Did anyone need to talk more?

Pictures, Pictures, Pictures

Focus: non-personal
Time: 15 minutes
Materials: mounted magazine pictures; paper; pens or pencils

For this activity you will have to bring to class a large selection of magazine pictures mounted on construction paper. You will need 20 pictures for each group. Number or letter each picture.

Divide students into groups of no more than five students each and distribute the pictures. Explain that students are to look at the pictures and classify them according to their common features or characteristics (for example, pictures of a bear, a cat, a dog, and a pig can all be classified as *animals*).Instruct students to appoint a secretary to write down the different classification words and the numbers of the pictures that belong under each of them.

When all groups have finished classifying, have one group display one set of its pictures so that the other students can guess what features or special characteristics those pictures have in common.

Word Search

Focus: non-personal
Time: 10 minutes
Materials: chalkboard and chalk; paper; pens or pencils

Divide the class into groups of three to five students each. Write a polysyllabic English word on the board; for example, *encyclopedia* or *translation*. Then explain that students will have three minutes to identify as many words as possible that can be derived from your original word. Each group should appoint a secretary to write down the group's words. Each correct word is worth one point.

At the end of the time limit, ask the groups to read their words to each other, allowing other groups to challenge any word read. If a group is challenged and the word is incorrect and/or does not appear in a dictionary in any form, the challenging group gets the point. The group with the greatest number of points at the end wins.

Changes in Meaning
Focus: non-personal
Time: 20 minutes
Materials: chalkboard and chalk;
exercise sheet, p. 83

Write the following sentence on the board:

She's not home.

Ask individual students to read the sentence, using different intonation patterns to convey these four meanings: anger, apology, uncertainty (question), and sadness. Point out that often it is not *what* we say but *how* we say it that is important.

Divide the class into groups of four or five students each and distribute copies of the exercise sheet. Review the activity directions and explain the five types of statements. Stress that sentences may represent more than one type of statement. Complete the activity with a large group sharing of answers.

What Does It Mean?
Focus: non-personal
Time: 20 minutes
Materials: pens or pencils;
exercise sheet, p. 84

Arrange the class in groups of three to five students each and distribute copies of the exercise sheet. Review the activity directions and stress that students may *not* use their dictionaries while the activity is in progress.

When all groups have finished their task, have them share their ideas with the class before they look up definitions in their dictionaries. You may repeat this activity many times by substituting new words. If a student knows a word, have him or her explain it to the others in his or her group.

Sage Advice and Home Remedies
Focus: non-personal
Time: 20 minutes
Materials: pens or pencils;
exercise sheet, p. 85

Divide the class into groups of four or five students each and distribute copies of the exercise sheet. Review the activity directions and the two examples. At the end of the time limit, ask students to share their "remedies" with the class.

Wedding Bells
Focus: non-personal
Time: 30 minutes
Materials: chalkboard and chalk;
paper; pens or pencils;
exercise sheets, pp. 86–87

Arrange the class in groups of three or four students each and distribute copies of Picture A, p. 86. Allow students eight minutes to brainstorm at least 10 reasons why people get married. Have each group appoint a secretary to write down the group's ideas. As an incentive, offer a prize to the group that presents the most reasons.

At the end of the time limit, have one group read its list to the class while you write that group's ideas on the board. Ask the other groups if they have anything to add to the board list. Encourage discussion of personal or cultural differences and similarities.

Distribute copies of Picture B, p. 87 and this time have students brainstorm at least 10 reasons why married people fight. As before, have one group share its list with the class while you write their reasons on the board.

As a follow-up, ask students to work in pairs to write a dialog between the two people pictured on either exercise sheet A or B. If time permits and there is interest, have students read their dialogs to the class.

Strategy 5
Small Group Activities

Who Married Whom?

Focus: non-personal
Time: 20 minutes
Materials: exercise sheet, p. 88

Divide the class into groups of three or four students each and distribute copies of the exercise sheet. Review the activity directions. Allow students to work alone first, reading and discussing the problem. If they seem to have difficulty approaching the task, read the following clues and instruct students to cross off the individual names as they receive more information.

Clues

Bill was engaged to Jane but ended up with the woman who later became a model. This means he did not marry Jane.

Frances became a computer technician and married a college president who was not her college sweetheart. This means that she did not marry Bill or Charlie.

Mary became a teacher.

Only one man married his college sweetheart.

Allow students time to reach their own conclusions based on the clues. Then read the following solution:

Solution

Bill married Carol.
Charlie married Jane.
Frank married Frances.
Jim married Mary.

News Stories

Focus: non-personal
Time: 20 minutes
Materials: pens or pencils;
exercise sheets, pp. 89–90

Divide the class into groups of five students each and distribute copies of the exercise sheet, p. 89. Assign half the groups to be reporters and half the groups to be characters or witnesses in the story. (If you have more than 10 students in your class, you may want to add more characters to the story and assign more students to be reporters and witnesses.) Read the activity directions aloud and explain the meaning of the words *reporter* and *witness* if necessary.

After students have read the story, have the reporters interview one character or witness each for three to five minutes, using the questions on the exercise sheet, p. 90.

Encourage students acting as witnesses to use their imaginations.

When the reporters have finished interviewing all the characters, allow them five more minutes to organize their information before they report their findings to the class.

As a follow-up, ask students to bring in real news items and to write their own stories.

Starting Over

    Focus: non-personal
    Time: 30 minutes
    Materials: chalkboard and chalk; paper;
          pens or pencils;
          exercise sheet, p. 91.

Divide the class into groups of three to five students each and distribute copies of the exercise sheet. Review the activity directions and tell the groups they will have 20 minutes to solve the problem.

When the groups have completed their survivors lists, have one student from each group write that group's list on the board. Ask the other group members to provide information about each of the survivors. Encourage questions.

As a follow-up the next day, have the groups compare their results. List on the board the different answers to the following questions:

What occupations do the survivors represent?
How old are the survivors?
Can all of the survivors produce children?
What religions are represented, if any?
What nationalities are the survivors?

The Desert Island

    Focus: non-personal
    Time: 30 minutes
    Materials: paper; pens or pencils;
          exercise sheet, p. 92.

Divide the class into groups of three to five students each and distribute copies of the exercise sheet. Review the activity directions and answer any questions. Stress the importance of group cooperation and the need for complete agreement or consensus. When everyone has understood the story and task, allow students 20 minutes to create their lists.

Thinking and Feeling

    Focus: personal
    Time: 15 minutes
    Materials: pens or pencils; paper;
          exercise sheets, pp. 93–94

Use the exercise sheets provided or create your own. Divide the class into groups of three or five students each and distribute copies of each exercise sheet. Review the activity directions. As a follow-up, have students expand upon their feelings by writing a short paragraph (or a composition) beginning with one of the sentences on the exercise sheet.

Changes in Meaning

Directions: Study the different types of statements and their abbreviations below. Then, with your group, read each numbered sentence and decide what type of statement it is and when or where it might be used. There can be more than one correct answer for each statement. Sentence 1 is an example.

Types of Statements
Future Statement = FS
Command Statement = CS
Experience Statement = ES
Rule Statement = RS
Private Statement = PS

1. There are 365 days in a year. **RS**
2. Bill's mother has blonde hair.
3. Sue is a pretty young woman.
4. I am going to Mexico next summer.
5. Sit down.
6. Pull your chairs into a circle.
7. It is 5 o'clock.
8. If you will open the window, you will feel better.
9. The movie begins at 9 o'clock.
10. Smoking causes lung cancer.
11. It costs 22¢ to send a letter in the United States.
12. The papers are in the office.
13. The book is brown.
14. Add 1 teaspoon of flour.
15. Your coat is dirty.
16. If you would wash your car, it would look better.
17. He was born in 1949.
18. Thirty-six inches make one yard.
19. I have a headache.
20. I like your new suit.

What Does It Mean?

Directions: Read the English words listed below. Do you know their meanings? With your group, decide on the meaning of each word and its part of speech. Write sample sentences using each word. If you do not know what the word means, *invent* a meaning and write a sentence. Use your imagination. Do not use your dictionary!

Word	Part of Speech	Definition	Sentence
1. quash	_____	_____	_____
			_____
2. propinquity	_____	_____	_____
			_____
3. jalousie	_____	_____	_____
			_____
4. grackle	_____	_____	_____
			_____
5. flurry	_____	_____	_____
			_____
6. meddle	_____	_____	_____
			_____
7. ravenous	_____	_____	_____
			_____
8. stave	_____	_____	_____
			_____

Sage Advice and Home Remedies

Directions: Read the health problems listed below. With your group, invent a cure or remedy for each problem and complete each sentence. Look at the first two examples, then use your imagination to complete the remaining sentences.

1. If you catch a cold, fry some onions, mix them with turpentine, and spread them on your chest.

2. If you get the chicken pox, lie on the floor of a chicken house and get somebody to chase a flock of chickens over you.

3. If you get the hiccoughs, _____

   _____

4. If your hair begins to fall out, _____

   _____

5. If you have flat feet, _____

   _____

6. If you want to stop smoking, _____

   _____

7. If you want to grow tall, _____

   _____

8. If you want to lose weight, _____

   _____

9. If you want to find a boyfriend or girlfriend, _____

   _____

10. If you want to remember people's names, _____

    _____

Wedding Bells

Directions: Look at the two people in the picture below. They are going to get married next week. With your group, think of at least 10 possible reasons for these people to get married. Appoint a secretary to write your group's reasons on the lines provided. The group with the greatest number of reasons wins.

Picture A

1. _____
2. _____
3. _____
4. _____
5. _____
6. _____
7. _____
8. _____
9. _____
10. _____
11. _____
12. _____
13. _____

Continued

Look Who's Talking! ©1995 by Alta Book Center Publishers
Permission is granted to reproduce this page for classroom use.

Wedding Bells Continued

Directions: Look at the two people in the picture below. They are married, but they are not very happy right now. With your group, think of at least 10 possible reasons why these people are fighting. Appoint a secretary to write your group's reasons on the lines provided. The group with the greatest number of reasons wins.

Picture B

1. _____

2. _____

3. _____

4. _____

5. _____

6. _____

7. _____

8. _____

9. _____

10. _____

11. _____

12. _____

13. _____

Who Married Whom?

Directions: Read the story below and with your group try to decide which man married which woman. Your teacher will give you some clues if you need help. Make notes and write your answers on the lines provided.

Problem

Jane, Carol, Frances, Mary, Bill, Frank, Jim, and Charlie were all friends in college. They all married one another. Bill was engaged to Jane, but ended up with the woman who later became a model. Jim and Mary and Frances and Charlie were college sweethearts. Frances became a computer technician and married a college president who was not her college sweetheart. Mary became a teacher. Only one man married his college sweetheart. Can you figure out who married whom?

Solution

1. Bill married _____.

2. Charlie married _____.

3. Frank married _____.

4. Jim married _____.

Look Who's Talking! ©1995 by Alta Book Center Publishers
Permission is granted to reproduce this page for classroom use.

News Stories

Directions: Read the news story below and wait for your teacher to assign you a role. If you are a "reporter," use the questions on p. 90 to get information about the robbery. If you are a "witness," use your imagination to provide as much information as possible.

Bank Robbery

The Midtown Bank was robbed yesterday at 2:00 P.M. The bank robber was seen leaving the bank by Mr. James, who was shot in the leg. The getaway car was seen in the parking lot by Mrs. Peterson, who was hit as the car sped away. She was not seriously injured. Two bank tellers, Mr. Anderson and Ms. Wilson, talked with the robber, but they were unable to stop him. The police officer got a good, clear view of the robber and was able to give a complete description.

Continued

Directions: Ask one of the five characters, or witnesses, these questions. Write any information you receive on the lines provided.

Questions for the Reporter

1. What color were the robber's eyes?

   _____

2. What color was his hair?

   _____

3. What kind of gun did he have?

   _____

4. What was the robber wearing?

   _____

5. How tall was he?

   _____

6. About how much did he weigh?

   _____

7. Did the robber have any unusual characteristics or markings?

   _____

8. Can you describe the getaway car?

   _____

9. Was the robber alone?

   _____

10. What was his voice like? Did he have any sort of accent?

    _____

11. In which direction did he go?

    _____

12. What did he say during the robbery?

    _____

Starting Over

Directions: Read the news flash below. Then try to solve the problem with your group, using the questions provided as a guide. Write your list on a separate sheet of paper. Everyone in your group must agree on the solution.

NEWS FLASH!

The civilized world has been destroyed by mysterious moon rays. Ten people have survived and managed to find shelter. The shelter has only enough food and water for *seven* people.

With your group, make a list of the seven people who should remain in the shelter (the other three will go for help but they will not survive). Think about and discuss who would be the ideal people to help the human race start over and what society needs in order to survive. Everyone in your group must agree on the seven people selected. When making your list, consider answers to the following questions:

1. What are the people's names?

2. How old are they?

3. What occupations do they have?

4. Do they have any physical limitations?

5. Can they produce children?

6. What are their political views?

7. What are their religious views?

8. What are their educational backgrounds?

9. What are their nationalities?

The Desert Island

Directions: Read the story below. Then try to solve the problem with your group, using the lists of items provided. Write your final list on a separate sheet of paper. Everyone in your group must agree on the solution.

Story

You are on a sinking ship with a group of friends. Rubber lifeboats are available, but the boats can hold only a limited number of people and supplies. You see a desert island in the distance. If your boat makes it to the island, you will need certain supplies to help you survive.

Problem

You can only take 18 items with you in your boat, three from each of the six groups below. Look at the lists of items and with your group decide which items you will take and which ones you will leave behind. Everyone in your group must agree on the same items. Work as a group, not individually.

Group 1
large flares
matches
flashlights
oil lamps
oil
batteries
can opener
utensils

Group 2
pillows
sleeping bags
tent
blankets
sheets
coats and jackets
extra clothes

Group 3
fresh water
soda
coffee
canned juices
beer
tea
whiskey

Group 4
salt
flour
sugar
yeast
powdered milk
water purification tablets

Group 5
bows and arrows
knives
gun
bullets
fishing pole
small chairs
dishes
first-aid kit
ropes

Group 6
frozen meat
dried fruits
dried vegetables
fresh fruits
fresh vegetables
canned beans
dried soup

Thinking and Feeling

Directions: With your group, think of as many words as you can that describe feelings. Write the words on the lines provided. A few words are given as examples.

sad
_____   _____   _____   _____

happy
_____   _____   _____   _____

nervous
_____   _____   _____   _____

sleepy
_____   _____   _____   _____

_____   _____   _____   _____

_____   _____   _____   _____

_____   _____   _____   _____

_____   _____   _____   _____

Continued

Thinking and Feeling Continued

Directions: With your group, finish the sentences below.
Listen carefully as your classmates describe their feelings or
emotions. Write your own feelings on the lines provided.

When I get up in the morning, I feel _____

When I get a good grade on a test, I feel _____

When someone understands my English well, I feel _____

When I don't get enough sleep, I feel _____

When I go to the dentist, I feel _____

When I fight with a friend, I feel _____

When someone is rude to me, I feel _____

When someone gives me a present, I feel _____

When I don't have any money, I feel _____

When I listen to romantic music, I feel _____

When I lose something, I feel _____

When _____ , I feel _____

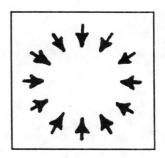

Strategy 6
Large Group

The Ideal Partner
  Focus: non-personal
  Time: 45 minutes
  Materials: 4–5 mounted magazine pictures
    or photos of faces

Before class, mount four or five magazine pictures or photos on large sheets of newsprint or butcher paper. Next to each picture, list some characteristics or traits of that person, as shown in the following examples:

Marcy	Gus
beautiful	hardworking
sexy	no education
bad housekeeper	good father
rich	good sense of humor
faithful to husband	very quiet
a little lazy	religious
affectionate	likes TV

Hang the sheets around the room and discuss the different people with your students, asking questions such as, What are this person's "good" qualities? What traits might be hard to live with? Have students select, from the pictures, someone to be their husband or wife. Students must explain their choices.

Then, divide the class into two groups—men in one and women in the other—and assign the groups to different corners of the room. Have each group brainstorm a list of important qualities for a prospective partner to possess. After 15 minutes, reconvene the class and ask the groups to share their lists. Find out what the men think of the women's list. Is it fair? Are the qualities listed "important"? Do the men feel something is missing from the women's list? Ask the women to evaluate the men's list in the same way.

Next, if interest is high, have each student rank in order three important characteristics to look for in a mate. After a few minutes, survey the men and women to see if there is any consensus.

As a wrap-up, ask your students to consider how many of the qualities they listed could be ascribed to themselves. Are they looking for someone who is like them? Or are they looking for someone who is very different from them, someone who would complement them? Share answers with the class.

Grab Bag
  Focus: non-personal
  Time: 15 minutes
  Materials: a large paper bag;
    1 personal item from each student

Several days before you undertake this activity, ask each student to bring to class a small, unbreakable item. The item should be small enough to fit in a large paper bag with all the other items that students bring.

For the activity have students take turns picking an item out of the bag and showing it to the class. The other students should try to guess who brought in the item and why they believe their guess is correct. After one or two minutes of guessing per item, find out to whom the item really belongs.

Five Good Minutes
  Focus: personal
  Time: 20 minutes
  Materials: chalkboard and chalk

Ask students to review their past 24 hours—where they have been, whom they have seen, what they have been doing. Allow two or three minutes for students to think of five minutes that were particularly enjoyable. Then, moving quickly around the room, ask each student to share his or her "five good minutes." Write the responses on the board.

When everyone has responded, have the class determine what factors contribute to one's enjoyment—what kinds of things tend to make life worthwhile. See what ideas emerge and if there are any commonalities in the students' responses. Discuss with students how they could incorporate more "good minutes" into their lives. What would they have to do or what would the circumstances have to be? Do they foresee more enjoyment in the future? Why or why not?

Fun Under $5.

   Focus: non-personal
   Time: 10 minutes
   Materials: chalkboard and chalk;
      paper;
      pens or pencils

Ask your student to brainstorm the number of fun things they can do for under five dollars in their new (American) city. Appoint a class secretary to write students' ideas on the board, no matter how crazy they may seem.

When the board list is complete, ask various students whether or not they have done any of the things listed or whether they would like to do them. Notice which activities interest which students. Suggest that the class make a social calendar in order to schedule outings together. Have one student assemble a list of the students' names and phone numbers and/or addresses. Find out who has a car, who doesn't, who is over 21 years of age (if drinking is anticipated).

This activity is an excellent way to unite the class socially and to provide students with occasions to practice their English outside the classroom.

Polar Opposites—By Degree

   Focus: personal
   Time: 20 minutes
   Materials: magazine pictures or photos of people

In opposite corners of the classroom, display magazine pictures or photos representing two people with opposite points of view on a particular topic. (See the topics list and character descriptions in the next column.) Describe in detail the viewpoints of these two characters, making certain that students understand the differences of opinion. Exaggerate the characters as much as necessary.

Then have students imagine a line running down the center of the classroom, each pole representing one extreme of opinion on the topic. Instruct students to stand on the "line" at a point that best represents their own position or viewpoint regarding the topic. Students will need to talk to one another to determine where they should stand.

When everyone has found a place on the line, have students recall a recent or past experience that might have influenced their choice of position. Then have students pair up with someone at the opposite end of the line to compare the reasons for their respective points of view.

Here are some suggestions for controversial topics, followed by sample character descriptions to accompany the magazine pictures or photos:

Topics

TV fanatic vs. TV hater
Avid letter writer vs. Non-letter writer
Sociable, friendly person vs. Loner
Quick-tempered person vs. Calm person
Very religious person vs. Non-believer
Spender vs. Saver
Student vs. Loafer
Health food advocate vs. Junk food eater

Character Descriptions

A. Plug-It-In-Paul is crazy about electrical appliances and gadgets. In his bedroom alone he has an electric clock, a radio, an electric blanket, and a bed that gives a massage with just the flip of a switch. In addition, he has an automatic pajama folder and a closet door that is operated by an electric eye. He pushes a button and an electric current opens and closes the drawers in his dresser. He has automatic curtain pulls, an electric carpet heater, and an electric slipper warmer. His pillow turns automatically every 23 minutes, and when it is time to get up in the morning, he is awakened by the electronic melodies produced by his two synthesizers.

B. Back-to-Nature-Nancy cooks over an open fire. She entertains herself at night reading by a kerosene lamp and playing her guitar. She keeps her milk cold in an old ice chest and wouldn't dream of drying her hair any other way but in the sunlight. She has a wind-up clock and a rusty bicycle she rides to work at the local feed and grain store. She doesn't own an iron or use any electricity. She washes her clothes by hand.

Choosing Sides

Focus: non-personal
Time: 15 minutes
Materials: a list of characteristics or symbols

Prepare ahead of class a list of opposing characteristics or symbols. (See suggestions below.) Explain that students will be asked to choose from two characteristics or symbols, the one that best describes them, and to then go stand on the side of the room that represents their choice. Offer the following question as an example:

Are you a station wagon or a sports car?
(all station wagons go to one corner; all sports cars go to another corner)

Tell students that they must make a choice. Nobody may stand in the middle of the room.

When all students have chosen sides, ask three or four students from each side to tell the others why they chose the side they did. Pose questions such as these:

What's it like being a(n) . . . ?
How do you know that you are a(n) . . . ?
Tell me about . . . .
Are you glad that you are a(n) . . . ? Why?
How long have you been a(n) . . . ?
What's the advantage of being a(n) . . . ?

Each time you present the activity, offer three or four different sets of symbols so that students can move back and forth across the room, associating with different students according to their choices. With each set, elicit responses to the types of questions presented above.

As a follow-up, ask students to form dyads or small groups to share opinions or feelings suggested by the activity. Some students might like to write about how they felt or what they discovered during the activity.

Here are some ideas for characteristics and symbols:

Are you a why or a why not?
Are you a watch-it-done or a do-it-yourself?
Are you a loud speaker or a private phone?
Are you a screen door or an open window?
Are you a pussycat or a tiger?
Are you a dancing shoe or a jogging shoe?
Are you a sunrise or a sunset?
Are you a throw-it-away-and-buy-a-new-one or a fix-up-the-old-one?

Are you a cold shower or a hot tub?
Are you a *Wall Street Journal* or a comic book?
Are you a do-it-now or an it-can-wait?
Are you a fancy-dress-and-the-Hilton or a jeans-and-camping?
Are you a make-a-list or a where-am-I?
Are you white gloves or dusty boots?

Upsies and Downsies

Focus: personal
Time: 20 minutes
Materials: exercise sheet, p. 101

For this activity you need to allow plenty of time for thought gathering. Encourage students to ask questions of one another and share your own experiences first, offering personal examples.

Distribute copies of the exercise sheet and review the definitions of *upsy* and *downsy*. Give several examples of people and things that have been upsies or downsies for you. Then have students work alone on the exercise sheet for 10 minutes. At the end of the time limit, review the questions and ask students to share their answers if they wish.

Missing Parts

Focus: non-personal
Time: 15 minutes
Materials: chalkboard and chalk;
exercise sheets, p. 102–103

Divide the class into groups of 7 to 10 students each and have each group appoint a secretary. Distribute copies of Picture A and allow students to look at the picture for about one minute. Then collect the sheets and distribute copies of Picture B. Have students look at the new picture for another minute.

Students should then take turns reporting to their secretary any parts or items that are missing from Picture B that were present in Picture A. Ask each group's secretary to come to the board and write his or her group's list of missing items.

As a wrap-up, redistribute copies of Picture A and have students see how many of the missing parts or items they correctly identified.

Answers: From left to right, some wallpaper stripes, a flower, the fork, the globe, the light bulb, the window bars, and the fish are missing.

Keeping Journals
    Focus: personal
    Time: 25 minutes
    Materials: paper; staples; colored pens or
           pencils; pens or pencils;
           exercise sheet, p. 104

This activity involves students initially in constructing their own journals for subsequent writing activities. Journals for each student can be made by cutting in half 15 sheets of $8\frac{1}{2}$" x 11" paper and stapling the half-sheets together in book form. Students can then decorate their journal covers.

On the days that you plan to do journal writing, distribute the journals and copies of the exercise sheet. Explain to students that they will be interviewing each other during the following weeks, using the questions on their exercise sheets. Let students know that you will collect their journals and read what they have written because you are interested. You may want to make comments in the journals, but avoid correcting errors of grammar or content.

Divide the class into student pairs and allow students 8 to 10 minutes for each interview. Be sure that students begin each interview by writing their classmate's name at the top of a new page. Follow up each interview with a large group sharing and continue the activity until all students have had a chance to interview and be interviewed by one another. In the large group sharing, have students tell what they found out about their classmates.

Encourage questions when students don't understand something or want additional information. The large group sharing allows students to build their own confidence by presenting information to a group in a structured way.

Families and Home Life
    Focus: personal
    Time: 25 minutes
    Materials: paper; pens or pencils;
           exercise sheet, p. 105

Divide the class into groups of 8 to 12 students each and distribute copies of the exercise sheet. Review the activity directions and have students appoint a secretary to write down the group's responses. Follow up with a large group sharing.

Horse Traders
    Focus: non-personal
    Time: 15 minutes
    Materials: pens or pencils;
           exercise sheet, p. 106

Divide the class into groups of 7 to 10 students each and distribute copies of the exercise sheet. Review the activity directions and allow students 5 to 10 minutes to find a solution.

We're Just Alike
    Focus: non-personal
    Time: 15–20 minutes
    Materials: exercise sheet, p. 107

Distribute copies of the exercise sheet and have students look at the word lists presented. Read the following examples:

    penny, car, and toaster are all made of metal
    bread, apple, and ice cream are all things to eat

Ask students to look for groups of words that have things in common. Any combination of words will do as long as the words share at least one characteristic. Each group must have a minimum of three words.

Sink or Float
    Focus: non-personal
    Time: 25 minutes
    Materials: objects that either sink or float;
           a large, clear plastic container;
           water or water source; pens or pencils;
           exercise sheet, p. 108

For this activity you need to collect a variety of objects that will either sink or float in water. Fill a large, clear plastic container with water and distribute copies of the exercise sheet. Review the activity directions. Have the students share their answers at the end of class.

Upsies and Downsies

Directions: Read the following definitions and listen as your teacher gives you some examples. Then answer the questions and, if you wish, share your experiences with the class.

An "upsy" is something or someone who has made you feel good.

A "downsy" is something or someone who has made you feel bad.

1. Recall someone who was an upsy for you. Think about the way the person made you feel.

2. Recall someone who was a downsy for you. Think about the way the person made you feel.

3. Think about the last time you were an upsy for someone else. What did you do? How did you feel? What did they do? How did they feel?

4. Think about the last time you were a downsy for someone else. What did you do? How did you feel? What did they do? How did they feel?

5. Think about things that have been downsies for you.

6. Think about things that have been upsies for you.

Missing Parts

Directions: With your group, study this picture. Try to remember what you see. No writing allowed!

Picture A

Continued

Missing Parts Continued

Directions: With your group, study this picture. It is the same as the first picture, but some things are missing. What are they? Tell your group secretary what things you can't find.

Picture B

Keeping Journals

Directions: Use these questions to interview your classmates. For each interview, use a new journal page and write your classmate's name at the top.

1. How do you spell your name?

2. Where have you lived during your lifetime?

3. How long have you been in the United States and how long do you plan to stay here?

4. Where would you want to live if you could live anywhere in the world?

5. How many brothers and sisters do you have?

6. Where are your parents and what are they like?

7. Are you married? Do you have children?

8. Do you want to get married someday and have children?

9. Are you studying other things besides English?

10. What kind of work would you like to have if you could do whatever you wanted?

11. What do you do for fun, when you are not working or studying?

12. Do you have a religion that is the same religion as your parents?

13. What kind of American food do you eat?

14. Are you interested in politics? Do you follow the daily news?

15. What are the best and worst things about the United States for you?

16. Do you speak more than two languages?

17. What kind of music do you like to listen to?

18. Do you play a musical instrument?

19. How would you spend $500 if you found it under a rock?

20. What is the bravest thing you ever have done?

Families and Home Life

Directions: With your group, take turns sharing answers to
the following questions about your family and early home life.

1. While you were growing up, who did most of the household chores in your home?

2. Did your mother work outside your home—in a store or an office, for example?

3. Did you have assigned duties each day as you were growing up?
   If yes, what were they?

4. Do you remember being punished for doing wrong things?
   If yes, how did your parents punish you?

5. Did you have a lot of toys?

6. What was your favorite plaything as a child?

7. Did your mother or father sing or tell stories to you at bedtime?
   Do you remember the songs or stories?

8. Did your parents or brothers and sisters help you with your homework?

9. Did your family pray together at mealtime or at any other time?

10. Was religion an important part of your family life?

11. Did you go home for lunch during the school day?
    Was your father home for lunch too?

12. What kinds of things did your family like to do together?

Horse Traders

Directions: With your group, read the following story and answer the questions at the bottom of the page.

Story

Mr. Jones originally bought his horse, Charlie, for $300. He sold him to Mr. Smith for $350. Mr. Smith gave him $300 in cash with the promise that he would pay the remaining $50 within the month. Before Mr. Smith could pay Mr. Jones, Mr. Smith sold Charlie to Peter for $350. Peter gave Mr. Smith $250 with the promise to pay the $100 balance soon. Mr. Jones then wanted to buy Charlie back. He offered Peter $300. Peter accepted. Peter was happy because he made $50 and Mr. Jones had his horse back for the same price he paid in the first place.

Is Mr. Jones correct? Is Peter correct? What about Mr. Smith? What is wrong with the end of this story?

Mark (X) the best answer to each of these questions:

1. Who should be happiest with the results of the horse trading?

   _____ Mr. Jones.

   _____ Mr. Smith.

   _____ Peter.

2. Who should disagree with the final horse trade?

   _____ Mr. Jones.

   _____ Mr. Smith.

   _____ Peter.

3. Who owes money?

   _____ Mr. Jones.

   _____ Mr. Smith.

   _____ Peter.

We're Just Alike

Directions: Read the word lists below. Try to group together items from all the lists that have something in common, items that are alike in some way (for example, *ice cream, apple,* and *bread* are all *things to eat*). Each group must have at least three words.

penny	notebook	car	television
apple	radio	pen	newspaper
city	window	airplane	toaster
milk	bus	typewriter	flashlight
flower	bread	ice cream	crayon
cup	roller skates	tree	sun
spoon	knife	grass	fork
tomato	mountain	watch	telephone
map	envelope	fire	stamp
shoe	book	ring	desert

Sink or Float

Directions: Your teacher will bring to class a variety of objects that either sink or float in water. Examine the objects one by one and try to predict which ones will sink and which ones will float. As your teacher drops each object into the water, complete the chart below. Be prepared to share your answers with the class.

Object	Sink / Float	Reason

Teacher's Notes
& Reactions